D-DAY
AND THE
NORMANDY
CAMPAIGN

D-DAY AND THE NORMANDY CAMPAIGN

David Reisch, Editor

STACKPOLE
BOOKS
celebrating **90** *years*
Guilford, Connecticut

STACKPOLE BOOKS

For L. K. S.

Published by Stackpole Books
An imprint of The Rowman & Littlefield Publishing Group, Inc.
4501 Forbes Blvd., Ste. 200
Lanham, MD 20706
www.rowman.com

Distributed by NATIONAL BOOK NETWORK
800-462-6420

Copyright © 2018 by The Rowman & Littlefield Publishing Group, Inc.
Photographs pages ii–vii courtesy of National Archives
Design and composition by TPC Ink, LLC

British Library Cataloguing in Publication Information available

Library of Congress Cataloging-in-Publication Data available

ISBN 978-0-8117-1993-3 (paperback)
ISBN 978-0-8117-6783-5 (e-book)

♾™ The paper used in this publication meets the minimum requirements of American National Standard for Information Sciences—Permanence of Paper for Printed Library Materials, ANSI/NISO Z39.48-1992.

Printed in the United States of America

Contents

Series Introduction

FOR MORE THAN NINETY YEARS, STACKPOLE BOOKS has been publishing the very best in military history, from ancient Rome to the modern Middle East, from foxhole to headquarters. We are proud to draw on that rich heritage—our decades of experience and expertise— in publishing this brand-new series, Battle Briefings. Intended as short overviews, these books aim to introduce readers to history's most important battles and campaigns— and, we hope, to provide a launching pad for further exploration of the endlessly fascinating nooks and crannies of military history.

THE
ROAD
TO
D-DAY

By the time of D-Day, June 6, 1944, the United States had been at war for two and a half years, Great Britain for more than four and a half.

From the German invasion of Poland in September 1939 through the Japanese attack on Pearl Harbor in December 1941, the British fought virtually alone, joined by its Commonwealth partners. In Norway, in France, in Africa, at sea, and in the skies, the British stood against Nazi Germany as most of Europe fell. Between July and October 1940, not long after Dunkirk and the escape of the British Expeditionary Force from the European continent, the Royal Air Force in "their finest hour" fought off Hitler's Luftwaffe in the Battle of Britain, a major defeat for Germany that forced Hitler to call off an amphibious invasion of England and which kept the British Isles available for building up forces and launching an invasion of the continent. Dunkirk and the Battle of Britain: two moments when Britain—and the fate of Europe— hung by a thread; two moments when Britain endured.

Though the United States was not yet in the war, in large part

St. Paul's Cathedral in London during a Luftwaffe raid, 1940. During the war's early years, Britain stood resolute against the Germans, a beacon of freedom in a world at risk of being overrun by totalitarianism. NATIONAL ARCHIVES

because of strong pro-neutrality sentiment among the American people, the foundation had long existed for American-British cooperation. Connected by a common language and political and cultural heritages, the two nations had shared a "special relationship" since the middle of the nineteenth century. At times wary and uneasy, especially as the United States grew in industrial and military power to challenge the British, that relationship had brought the U.S. into World War I on Britain's side (after a period of agonized neutrality) and was already drawing the two sides closer in this new war.

President Franklin Roosevelt and Prime Minister Winston Churchill shared aristocratic backgrounds and personal and professional interests in naval affairs (Roosevelt had been assistant secretary of the navy under Woodrow Wilson, while Churchill had served as First Lord of the Admiralty in 1911–15 and again in 1939–40). Churchill's mother was

What the Allies Were Fighting For: The Atlantic Charter

The President of the United States of America and the Prime Minister, Mr. Churchill, representing His Majesty's Government in the United Kingdom, being met together, deem it right to make known certain common principles in the national policies of their respective countries on which they base their hopes for a better future for the world.

First, their countries seek no aggrandizement, territorial or other;

Second, they desire to see no territorial changes that do not accord with the freely expressed wishes of the peoples concerned;

Third, they respect the right of all peoples to choose the form of government under which they will live; and they wish to see sovereign rights and self-government restored to those who have been forcibly deprived of them;

Fourth, they will endeavor, with due respect for their existing obligations, to further the enjoyment by all States, great or small, victor or vanquished, of access, on equal terms, to the trade and to the raw materials of the world which are needed for their economic prosperity;

Fifth, they desire to bring about the fullest collaboration between all nations in the economic field with the object of securing, for all, improved labor standards, economic advancement and social security;

Sixth, after the final destruction of the Nazi tyranny, they hope to see established a peace which will afford to all nations the means of dwelling in safety within their own boundaries, and which will afford assurance that all the men in all lands may live out their lives in freedom from fear and want;

Seventh, such a peace should enable all men to traverse the high seas and oceans without hindrance;

Eighth, they believe that all of the nations of the world, for realistic as well as spiritual reasons must come to the abandonment of the use of force. Since no future peace can be maintained if land, sea or air armaments continue to be employed by nations which threaten, or may threaten, aggression outside of their frontiers, they believe, pending the establishment of a wider and permanent system of general security, that the disarmament of such nations is essential. They will likewise aid and encourage all other practicable measure which will lighten for peace-loving peoples the crushing burden of armaments. ■

Sept 1939	Invasion of Poland
May–June 1940	Battle of France
July–Oct 1940	Battle of Britain
Dec 1940– Feb 1941	Operation Compass
Apr–Nov 1941	Siege of Tobruk
June 22, 1941	Germany invades Soviet Union
Aug 1941	Atlantic Charter
Sept 1941	Siege of Leningrad begins
Oct 1941– Jan 1942	Battle of Moscow
Dec 7, 1941	Pearl Harbor
Dec 11, 1941	Germany declares war on U.S.
April 1942	Bataan Death March
May 1942	Battle of the Coral Sea
May 1942	Battle of Corregidor
May–June 1942	Battle of Gazala
June 7, 1942	Battle of Midway

(continued)

of the war and attempted to work around his countrymen's isolationism to aid the British. If Churchill's sometimes lonely prescience—his early recognition of Hitler's threat and of the necessity of hitching his nation to the United States—and his steeliness in the face of Nazi aggression represent the twentieth century's great act of courage by a statesman, Roosevelt's careful circumvention of and influence on American national opinion remain one of that century's bravura political performances.

It is fun to be in the same decade with you."
➤ *Roosevelt to Churchill*

In 1940 the Roosevelt–Churchill friendship produced an exchange of American warships for base rights in British territory (the so-called destroyers-for-bases deal) and, more significantly, the Lend-Lease Act, a policy of giving more substantial—and more obviously non-neutral—aid to Britain and, ultimately, many other countries until the end of the war. In August 1941, before the United States even entered the war, Roosevelt and Churchill met at Placentia Bay in Newfoundland, where their meetings produced the Atlantic Charter, a document of common vision for the postwar world.

American, and the prime minister harbored a lifelong affinity for the United States and understood that country's rising power better than many. Roosevelt, an Anglophile like many in the American political class, swiftly recognized the stakes

If the United States was not already on a course toward more open alliance with Great Britain, December 7, 1941, made it a certainty. On that date of infamy, the Japanese attacked Pearl Harbor and other American installations in the Pacific, as well as British territory. Four days later, Hitler blundered by declaring war on the United States and making it possible for the U.S. government to fight not only Japan, the enemy which had attacked it, but also Germany, the enemy which Anglo-American leaders considered the more serious threat.

N **ever before has there been a greater challenge to life, liberty, and civilization."**

> ➤ *Roosevelt on Germany*

Mere weeks after Pearl Harbor, Roosevelt and Churchill met in Washington. At the First Washington Conference, also known as Arcadia, the United States and Britain agreed, most importantly, on a Europe-first strategy, created a Combined Chiefs of Staff to oversee joint military decision-making, and agreed to invade North Africa within the year. (They also drafted documents that laid the groundwork for the United Nations.) Shortly thereafter, the U.S. also agreed to a buildup of forces in Britain, code-named Bolero, in preparation for a proposed cross-Channel invasion of France in 1943, known as Operation Roundup.

Events Before D-Day	
Aug 1942	Dieppe Raid
Aug 1942– Feb 1943	Guadalcanal Campaign
Oct–Nov 1942	Second Battle of El Alamein
Oct 1942– Feb 1943	Battle of Stalingrad
Nov 1942	Operation Torch
Feb 1943	Battle of Kasserine Pass
March 1943	Battle of the Mareth Line
May 1943	Axis surrender in Tunisia
July–Aug 1943	Sicilian Campaign
July–Aug 1943	Battle of Kursk
Jan 1944	Italian Campaign begins
Jan 1944	Siege of Leningrad lifted
March 1944	Battle of Imphal begins
April 1944	Battle of Kohima begins
June 4, 1944	Liberation of Rome

Led by the president and prime minister, the two sides met in June 1942, again in Washington, to formalize strategy. The Soviet Union had been at war with its former ally Germany for a year by that time. After punishing early battles, during which hundreds of thousands of Red Army troops had been taken prisoner, the Soviets halted the Germans at the gates of Moscow and gained a stronger grip on the war, but the tide on the Eastern Front had not yet turned. Opening a second front to aid the Russians was fore in the Allies' minds. The Americans were keen on the direct route: an invasion across the English Channel into France and thence into Germany. Having more than two years' experience fighting the Germans, having endured the frontal assaults of the last war (to say nothing of Churchill's involvement with the Gallipoli landings), and perhaps also keeping imperial considerations (i.e., the Suez Canal) in mind, the British favored a more indirect Mediterranean approach: Africa followed by Sicily and Italy, "the soft underbelly" of Europe, as Churchill put it. The British won out.

Pearl Harbor, December 7, 1941: the USS *Shaw* explodes. NATIONAL ARCHIVES

If we can agree on major purposes and objectives, our efforts will begin to fall in line and we won't be just thrashing around in the dark."

> *Eisenhower on Allied cooperation*

U.S. forces for the North African campaign were placed under the overall command of Dwight Eisenhower. Texas born, Kansas bred, and West Point educated, a chain-smoker whose famous grin concealed an infamous temper, Ike had missed out on overseas service in World War I, but he had served under prominent generals such as John Pershing, Douglas MacArthur, Fox Conner, and most importantly George Marshall, who recognized Ike's talent during a critical moment in world history. Since the outbreak of war in Europe, Eisenhower's rise had been meteoric, having been promoted to colonel in March 1941, to brigadier general six months later, to major general in March 1942, and to lieutenant general in July 1942. The man who would successfully—some have said he was the *only* general who could have done it—lead the Allies to victory in Europe had been a lieutenant colonel little more than three years before D-Day.

Eisenhower and Roosevelt in Sicily, December 1943. The president had found his man for the invasion of France. NATIONAL ARCHIVES

Americans under Eisenhower invaded North Africa—Morocco and Algeria—in November 1942 as part of Operation Torch. Though the landings and initial operations were not burdensomely difficult—complicated largely by diplomacy with the French, who had capitulated to Germany two years earlier—the Americans soon ran into the teeth of the German war machine: Erwin Rommel (the legendary Desert Fox) and his battle-hardened Afrika Korps, which mauled inexperienced and ill-led American troops at Kasserine Pass in February 1943.

Our people from the very highest to the very lowest have learned that this is not a child's game."

➤ *Eisenhower after Kasserine Pass*

The lessons were learned quickly, and Eisenhower—who confessed his personal responsibility for the disaster—fired the commander on the scene and elevated George Patton. Already one of the U.S. Army's rising-star field commanders, and personally eccentric (he believed in reincarnation), Patton had participated in the 1912

The Buildup

Brenton Wallace, an operations officer in Patton's Third Army, describes the buildup in England:

One of the biggest problems was the housing of the million-odd American troops. In solving this problem, we also worked closely with the British. They furnished the bulk of the accommodations, although some of the buildings were prefabricated ones brought from America and erected by our own Engineers. Our Engineers also built many complete air fields and roads. By the time all the American troops for the invasion had arrived, in addition to the Canadians and the British forces, every available building, new and old, was filled to capacity, many tent camps were in operation and thousands of troops were billeted on the populace.

The troops were divided into the Assault and the Build-Up forces. The Assault were the troops which made the actual assault landing across the beaches of Normandy. After these followed the Build-Up troops, which reinforced and maintained the Allied Expeditionary Forces.

All troops initially passed through the Concentration Area. For some time this might be their original home camp, for others a camp closer to the southern ports of England. From this Concentration Area, units moved by either rail or road to the Marshalling Areas. Units might remain here up to 2 weeks, usually 4 to 6 days. The final markings were completed, defective vehicles replaced, all vehicles were waterproofed so that they could land in salt water and not be ruined, and troops were broken down into unit parties and formed into craft loads.

From the Marshalling Areas, units then moved into the Embarkation Areas. This move was made under their own power over the roads, by craft or ship loads. In these Embarkation Areas were usually located a number of Embarkation Points—docks or improvised concrete docks for landing craft—called "Hards." In the Embarkation Area, final preparations were completed. Time there varied from a couple of hours to 2 days. There the troops were briefed, the Landing Ration (a type of K ration sufficient for 24 hours) and an Emergency Ration (chocolate reinforced with vitamins) were issued. A final hot meal was fed and the troops were ready to go aboard ship.

The time on shipboard was estimated as 48 hours, sometimes it was less. On shipboard Sea Passage Rations and vomit bags were issued.

The actual mileage from the ports of southern England to the beaches of Normandy was about 100 miles. ∎

(From *Patton and His Third Army*)

Olympics in fencing, chased Pancho Villa with the army in 1916, and was one of the early members of the U.S. Tank Corps. He had been wounded during World War I while commanding a tank offensive. He lacked the tact and diplomacy of a general like Eisenhower, but he had the special skill, though not always employed without controversy, of motivating the fighting man and inspiring fear in the enemy. Patton quickly rehabilitated American troops broken at Kasserine Pass, bringing in new doctrine, stronger training, and reinvigorated leadership.

If we die killing, well and good, but if we fight hard enough, viciously enough, we will kill and live. Live to return to our family and our girl as conquering heroes—men of Mars."
➤ *Patton upon taking command*

At El Guettar in Tunisia, this reborn fighting force defeated the battle-hardened Germans. Six weeks later, Tunisia fell to the Allies, a turning-point victory that netted more than 200,000 prisoners. It had been primarily a British success— the British had been fighting the Italians and Germans longer in Africa, driving them out of Egypt and scoring critical wins at El

North Africa: American troops land in Algeria as part of Operation Torch. The November 1942 offensive was the first major American effort in Europe, almost a year after Pearl Harbor and Hitler's subsequent declaration of war.
NATIONAL ARCHIVES

Alamein and elsewhere—but after early defeats, the U.S. was developing into a formidable fighting force. There was still much to learn—at bloody cost in men—but the U.S. Army was on the path toward combining battlefield prowess with industrial and numerical might. The Germans were starting to pay attention.

At the Casablanca Conference in January 1943, months before the conclusion of the North Africa campaign, the Allies met again: Churchill, Roosevelt, but still no Stalin. Here, at one of the war's most consequential summits, Roosevelt, borrowing from Ulysses Grant, insisted on the unconditional surrender of the Axis. Reluctantly,

Churchill and the British agreed; though the Americans had earlier compromised in agreeing to a Mediterranean strategy, growing American strength was making the United States a more dominant alliance partner. Waxing U.S. power was not enough, however, to secure an early cross-Channel invasion. Despite lobbying from Roosevelt and his military commanders, the British could not be persuaded. They pointed at Sicily, followed by Italy, for the next move, which could draw German forces down out of Europe into the Italian peninsula, away from the Red Army on the Eastern Front and away from the future (and unavoidable) Allied invasion in France. Sicily and Italy it

Allied Deception

B renton Wallace, who served under Patton, writes of the situation a few days after D-Day:

The Germans were breathing uneasily. Anxiously their High Command checked the reports from spies in England and from Intelligence Units in Normandy to discover what reserves the Allies had. They knew that one corps of General George S. Patton's Third Army, the VIII, had been attached to the First Army for the invasion, but that most of his Third Army were still in England. It was in connection with them that the second of the "greatest bluffs in history" occurred.

We knew that General Eisenhower, the Supreme Allied Commander, had the highest esteem for General Patton and his Third Army, and we had heard that the Germans, having felt his quality in Sicily, feared him greatly. But we did not then know why Third Army Headquarters was left near the little town of Knutsford, a few miles south of Manchester, and why our troops were scattered through England and North Ireland for more than three weeks after the invasion started.

It was part of the "cover plan," as it was called. Keeping General Patton and his army where they were, and being sure to let the German agents find out that they were there, constituted such a threat to Germany, and her leaders so feared a direct thrust by the Third Army at some other point, that they kept 17 divisions along the Pas de Calais section of the Channel coast, afraid to use them as reinforcements in Normandy.

So realistically was this cover plan carried out that each day ships on the east coast were loaded with troops and just at dusk they moved out into the Channel while it was still light enough for German observation planes to see them. Then, after darkness settled, they moved back again into port and unloaded.

Thus a double purpose was served. Troops and the crews of the ships had valuable training in quick loading and unloading, and a new battle had been won in the war of nerves we were waging against the Germans. They never could be sure whether it was just another bluff. In some cases where reinforcements actually were being sent to the First Army in Normandy the ships would move into the Channel just before dark as if heading for a new point of invasion, then under cover of darkness would change course to head for the Normandy beaches. By such deceptive measures, the Germans were fooled completely. ■

(From *Patton and His Third Army*)

An American B-17 Flying Fortress bombs an aircraft plant in Germany, October 1943.
NATIONAL ARCHIVES

would be, and Operation Roundup withered on the vine.

At Casablanca, the Americans and British also agreed to a plan for the Combined Bomber Offensive against German industrial targets, with special emphasis on aircraft factories and plants manufacturing items essential to aircraft, such as ball bearings and petroleum. This would keep fighters out of the sky during any invasion in France. The plan was executed later in 1943 as Operation Pointblank and included raids on industrial complexes such as Schweinfurt. Many of these raiding bombers suffered heavy losses to German fighters, a problem that would soon be addressed by an American longer-range fighter plane that could accompany the bombers to fight off the menacing German fighters.

> **I do have the feeling of a crusader in this war."**
>
> ➤ *Eisenhower*

Meanwhile, Americans were waging vigorous war in the Pacific, a theater that loomed large in the American people's minds and that had already produced major campaigns and required significant commitments of men and materiel —essential to the war against Japan but a draw from Europe. By the end of the campaign in Africa, the

THE ROAD TO D-DAY

The USS *Enterprise* at the Battle of Midway, a striking victory for the United States six months into the war. Above all it helped turn the tide against Japan, but the battle also helped sustain American morale. NATIONAL ARCHIVES

United States had already scored an important victory at Midway and won the Guadalcanal campaign, two of the Pacific War's turning points. Also in early 1943, and spelling bad news for the Axis, the Soviets had struck a shattering blow against the Germans on the Eastern Front in the five-month-long Battle of Stalingrad, with more than a million soldiers on each side participating and hundreds of thousands of casualties.

On July 9, 1943, Operation Husky began: the Allied invasion of Sicily. In a campaign lasting a month and a half and foreshadowing D-Day in its combination of amphibious and airborne assaults, American and British forces landed on separate parts of the island, and each made a drive toward Messina in Sicily's northeastern corner. Commanding the British task

force was Bernard Montgomery. Wounded in the First World War, Montgomery led a division in the Battle of France and proved instrumental in saving British forces at Dunkirk. Favoring sweaters and a black beret and traveling with his pet canaries and dogs, Monty had a reputation as an inspiring field commander and for an insulting personality. (At their first meeting earlier in the war, before Eisenhower was Montgomery's superior, Monty had insisted that Ike put out his cigarette.) Taking over the British Eighth Army in Africa, he turned it into the force that bested Rommel, a victory that made Monty the hero of El Alamein. In a "race" made famous by the movie *Patton*, the general beat Montgomery's British troops into Messina, while the Germans flowed across the straits into Italy.

Führer Directive No. 51:
November 1943

For the last two and one-half years the bitter and costly struggle against Bolshevism has made the utmost demands upon the bulk of our military resources and energies. This commitment was in keeping with the seriousness of the danger, and the over-all situation. The situation has since changed. The threat from the East remains, but an even greater danger looms in the West: the Anglo-American landing! In the East, the vastness of the space will, as a last resort, permit a loss of territory even on a major scale, without suffering a mortal blow to Germany's chance for survival.

Not so in the West! If the enemy here succeeds in penetrating our defenses on a wide front, consequences of staggering proportions will follow within a short time. All signs point to an offensive against the Western Front of Europe no later than spring, and perhaps earlier.

For that reason, I can no longer justify the further weakening of the West in favor of other theaters of war. I have therefore decided to strengthen the defenses in the West, particularly at places from which we shall launch our long-range war against England. For those are the very points at which the enemy must and will attack; there—unless all indications are misleading—will be fought the decisive invasion battle. . . .

During the opening phase of the battle, the entire striking power of the enemy will of necessity be directed against our forces manning the coast. Only an all-out effort in the construction of fortifications, an unsurpassed effort that will enlist all available manpower and physical resources of Germany and the occupied areas, will be able to strengthen our defenses along the coasts within the short time that still appears to be left to us. . . .

Should the enemy nevertheless force a landing by concentrating his armed might, he must be hit by the full fury of our counterattack. For this mission ample and speedy reinforcements of men and materiel, as well as intensive training must transform available larger units into first-rate, fully mobile general reserves suitable for offensive operations. The counterattack of these units will prevent the enlargement of the beachhead, and throw the enemy back into the sea.

In addition, well-planned emergency measures, prepared down to the last detail, must enable us instantly to throw against the invader every fit man and machine from coastal sectors not under attack and from the home front. ∎

Sicily: Matthew Ridgway and officers of the 82nd Airborne Division. The division suffered heavy casualties on the island. U.S. ARMY MILITARY HISTORY INSTITUTE

We are going to finish with this chap Rommel once and for all. It will be quite easy. There is no doubt about it. He is definitely a nuisance. Therefore we will hit him a crack and finish with him."

➤ *Montgomery, 1942*

Here, still higher field command lay within his grasp. (While Patton could not have filled Eisenhower's post successfully, the future field command of the American effort on D-Day and in Western Europe—a command that fell to Bradley— might have been his.) Until, that is, Patton slapped shell-shocked soldiers. It was a moment of supreme indiscretion and utter failure to understand modern combat's effect on soldiers, one that would dramatically influence the D-Day invasion and Normandy campaign.

The Mediterranean approach remains one of the controversial decisions of World War II, as it delayed the liberation of Western Europe, committed critical manpower to a tough war in Italy, and arguably subjected Allied strategy to the needs of the British Empire.

Left: Sicily: Patton converses with Lt. Col. Lyle Bernard of the 30th Infantry Regiment. NATIONAL ARCHIVES

Below: Sicily: Medics tend to a wounded soldier, August 1943. More than 2,800 Americans were killed and 6,400 wounded during the campaign. NATIONAL ARCHIVES

Nevertheless, the successful Allied invasion of Sicily precipitated the deposition of Benito Mussolini, who lost a vote of confidence in the third week of July 1943 and was ordered by the king to be arrested. Freed by German special forces in September, Mussolini was a discredited dictator, though he was not killed—and hung upside down—until a year and a half later. More than that, at the time of the Sicily offensive, the Germans launched a major attack on the Soviets—producing the

Dwight Eisenhower Career Highlights

1890	Born in Texas
1892	Moves to Kansas
1915	Graduates from West Point (61 of 164)
1918	Commands Camp Colt (Tank Corps), Gettysburg
1918–19	Infantry School
1922–24	Staff officer under Fox Conner, Panama
1926	Command and General Staff School (1 of 245)
1927–28	Army War College
1933–35	Aide to Army Chief of Staff MacArthur
1935–39	Adviser to MacArthur in Philippines
1940–41	Chief of Staff, 3rd Infantry Division
1941	Chief of Staff, IX Corps
	Chief of Staff, Third Army
	Promoted to brigadier general
1942	Deputy Chief, War Plans Division
	Chief, War Plans Division
	Assistant Chief of Staff, Operations, under Marshall
	Commander, European Theater of Operations (U.S.)
	Promoted to lieutenant general
1943	Promoted to full general
	Supreme Allied Commander, North Africa
	Supreme Allied Commander, Mediterranean
1943–45	Supreme Allied Commander, Europe
1944	Promoted to General of the Army
1945–48	Chief of Staff, U.S. Army
1948–50	President, Columbia University
1951–52	Supreme Allied Commander, Europe (NATO)
1953–61	President of the United States
1969	Died, Walter Reed Medical Center

Italy: a German plane smokes to the ground during the landings near Anzio, January 1944. U.S. NAVY

massive tank battle at Kursk—and some have since argued that operations on Sicily kept the Germans from fully reinforcing that offensive. Finally, there can be little doubt that fighting in Africa and then on Sicily gave the U.S. Army much-needed time to work itself into a respectable fighting force before D-Day.

A month after Sicily, in September, the Allies invaded Italy proper at Salerno (Operation Avalanche), with subsidiary operations at Calabria and Taranto. Allied attention was already shifting to France by this time. Eisenhower commanded the Avalanche offensive, but Omar Bradley, a valued subordinate of Eisenhower who had served under Patton on Sicily, was pulled out to plan the D-Day invasion and ultimately command the American ground portion of that offensive. Patton was gone, mired in controversy, but not hopelessly: his superiors would soon have other plans for him. By the time Allied forces landed at Anzio in January 1944 (Operation Shingle), Eisenhower had left for the Supreme Command.

Exercise Tiger, a dress rehearsal for D-Day on the beaches of England, April 1944.

Breaking out of Anzio and up the Italian peninsula would prove a tougher slog than anticipated. Rome eventually fell to the Americans on June 4, 1944, an event then and now overshadowed by what followed two days later, but the campaign in Italy would continue until the end of the war in Europe.

Allied commanders continued to meet. In August 1943, Churchill and Roosevelt met in Quebec for the Quadrant Conference, where they reaffirmed a May 1944 date for D-Day and endorsed the Over lord plan for the invasion, which Allied military planners had been working on since earlier that year. That plan focused on the coast of France east of the Cherbourg peninsula, an area that would provide the necessary beachheads on which to land troops and supplies. It was farther from England—and from the heart of Germany—than the other option, the Pas de Calais, but the Normandy beaches were believed to be less well defended than Calais and to be the Germans' less expected point of attack.

THE ROAD TO D-DAY

"Well, Ike, you are going to command Overlord."

> *Roosevelt to Eisenhower, December 1943*

At Tehran in late November 1943, the first meeting of the so-called Big Three—Roosevelt, Churchill, and Stalin—took place. Stalin enthusiastically welcomed the cross-Channel invasion, and any lingering British doubts over the operation were outvoted by the Americans and Russians. The offensive would be coordinated not only with an American-British invasion of southern France (Operation Dragoon, August 15), but also with a major Soviet attack on the Eastern Front (Operation Bagration, June 22).

Overlord now gathered momentum. By early 1944, the command structure of this vast undertaking was organized. Eisenhower commanded the entire effort—Supreme Headquarters Allied Expeditionary Force (SHAEF)—with a trio of British officers commanding the land, air, and sea components: Bernard Montgomery, Trafford

Bernard Montgomery Career Highlights

1887	Born in England
1908	Graduates from Royal Military Academy, Sandhurst
1914	Wounded in France
1916–18	Staff officer position on Western Front
1921–23	Chief of Staff, 17th Infantry Brigade (Irish Civil War)
1926–29	Deputy Assistant Adjutant General, Staff College, Camberley
1931	Commander, 1st Battalion, Royal Warwickshire (India, Palestine)
1937	Commander, 9th Infantry Brigade
1938	Commander, 8th Infantry Division (Palestine)
1939–40	Commander, 3rd Infantry Division (Battle of France)
1940	Commander, V Corps
1941	Commander, XII Corps
	Commander, South-Eastern Command
1942–43	Commander, Eighth Army
	Wins Second Battle of El Alamein
	Sicily and Italy campaigns
1944–45	Commander, 21st Army Group, which included all Allied ground forces for the D-Day invasion and the Normandy campaign, until September 1, when Eisenhower became overall ground commander, leaving Montgomery with a mostly British-Canadian army group stripped of the majority of its American divisions
Sept 1944	Operation Market Garden
1946–48	Chief of the Imperial General Staff
1951–58	Deputy Supreme Allied Commander Europe (NATO)
1976	Dies in England

Leigh-Mallory, and Bertram Ramsay, respectively. Ike's deputy would be another Briton, Arthur Tedder. Omar Bradley would lead the U.S. ground forces (First Army); Miles Dempsey would lead the Commonwealth contingent (Second Army).

The buildup of men and equipment continued, while training picked up pace and Allied air force missions in Europe intensified, now

American bombs strike German positions at Pointe du Hoc on the Normandy coast several weeks before D-Day. NATIONAL ARCHIVES

focusing on transportation networks in order to hinder the movement of German forces responding to the invasion. In May 1944, for example, as part of Operation Chattanooga Choo-Choo, Allied fighters targeted railroads and trains. The Allies were also conducting one of history's most successful deception operations. The indispensable Patton was put in charge of the fictional First U.S. Army Group (FUSAG) in southeastern England. Patton's name, false intelligence, and dummy tanks and landing craft convinced the Germans that the main attack would come at Calais. Historians debate the magnitude of the ruse's impact, but it was a deception that would have effects—positive for the Allies, negative for the Germans—well after D-Day. Meanwhile, Allied planners had settled on June 5 for the invasion—when the full moon allowed for visibility for the airborne drops.

> **You will enter the continent of Europe and, in conjunction with the other United Nations, undertake operations aimed at the heart of Germany and the destruction of her armed forces."**
> —*Eisenhower's orders, February 1944*

Gen. Omar Bradley and Adm. Alan Kirk during a rehearsal for the invasion. NATIONAL ARCHIVES

The stage was nearly set for the liberation of Western Europe and the final defeat of Nazi Germany, but before achieving those ends, the Allies would have to contend not only with geography and weather, but also with the Germans who had been entrenching themselves in France since 1942.

The German war machine had made quick work of Denmark, Norway, the Netherlands, Belgium, Luxembourg, and France in the spring of 1940. The perimeter of this vast territory was a coastline of more than 2,000 miles, stretching from north of the Arctic Circle in Norway, along the North Sea coast of Denmark, the Netherlands, and Belgium, along the English Channel coast of northern France, and along the Bay of Biscay coast of western France, terminating at the Spanish border. (Francisco Franco's Spain provided support in men and equipment to Nazi Germany but never formally allied with the Axis.)

We have to be on guard like a spider in its web."

➤ *Hitler, 1943*

Construction on the Atlantic Wall—part of Hitler's grand plan to turn the continent into *Festung Europa*, Fortress Europe—began in the middle of 1942 as a project of Organisation Todt, the engineering group that had built the Autobahn and the West Wall (Siegfried Line). In France, where the Germans expected the Allied invasion to take place, hundreds of thousands of

THE ROAD TO D-DAY

Above: Vessels gathering and loading in England before D-Day.
NATIONAL ARCHIVES

Below: Troops board landing craft in England. NATIONAL ARCHIVES

Loading equipment in the days before D-Day.
NATIONAL ARCHIVES

workers—most of them Frenchmen drafted into labor by the Vichy government, along with slave labor—poured 600 million cubic feet of concrete and laid more than a million tons of steel to create a coastal network of bunkers, pillboxes, gun turrets, and machine-gun nests.

In overall command of the soldiers who would man these fortifications, as well as those who would wait in reserve to pounce on any invasion, was Field Marshal Gerd von Rundstedt, German commander-in-chief in the West (OB-West). An aristocratic Prussian officer of the old school and a staff officer of the highest order, Rundstedt had been recalled from retirement to command an army group in Poland in 1939, France in 1940, and the

Soviet Union in 1941. Sixty-eight years old on D-Day, exhausted by four years of year, weakened by a heart attack in 1941, refused in his desire to retire, Rundstedt was the man tasked with defending against the Allied onslaught.

All this expenditure and effort was sheer waste."
➤ *Albert Speer, Third Reich minister for armaments and war production, on the Atlantic Wall*

Rundstedt had little faith in the Atlantic Wall, which he did not believe would stop the invaders—and, in any event, static defense was contrary to the German offensive spirit. The old field marshal argued

THE ROAD TO D-DAY

Gerd von Rundstedt Career Highlights

1875	Born in Germany
1893	Commissioned as lieutenant
1903–6	Kriegsakademie
1907–14	General Staff
1914	Chief of Staff, 22nd Division
1915	Chief of Staff, 86th Division
1916	Chief of Staff, XXV Reserve Corps
1917	Chief of Staff, LIII Corps
1918	Chief of Staff, XV Corps
1920	Chief of Staff, 3rd Cavalry Division
1926	Chief of Staff, Group Command 2
1928	Commander, 2nd Cavalry Division
1932	Commander, 3rd Infantry Division
	Commander, Group Command 1
1938	Army commander during Sudetenland crisis
	Retires
1939	Commander, Army Group South (Poland)
1940	Commander, Army Group A (France)
	Promoted to field marshal
	Plans aborted Operation Sealion
	Commander-in-Chief West
1941	Commander, Army Group South (Barbarossa)
	Dismissed but reinstated by Hitler after withdrawal from Rostov
1942–July 1944	Commander-in-Chief West (D-Day, Normandy)
1944	Heads Court of Honor after July 20 plot against Hitler
Sept 1944–45	Commander-in-Chief West (Siegfried Line, Ardennes, Rhine)
1945	Captured by Allies, accused of war crimes, never tried
1945–49	Imprisoned
1953	Dies in Germany

A German pillbox
defending the
Normandy beaches.
NATIONAL ARCHIVES

for a defense in depth, holding the valuable panzer forces in reserve, poised for a crushing counterattack once the Allies moved inland from the beaches.

Erwin Rommel, appointed by Hitler in early 1944 to command Army Group B under Rundstedt, disagreed, favoring the placement of the tanks closer to the beaches. Rommel was a different breed of soldier. Almost sixteen years younger than Rundstedt, the son of a teacher rather than Prussian nobility, Rommel had a fresher perspective on warfare. His years fighting in Africa, where he earned his field marshal's baton and his

Desert Fox nickname, taught Rommel an appreciation for combined-arms warfare, especially airpower and the threat aerial attacks would pose to Rundstedt's defense-in-depth approach.

He is an energetic and determined commander. . . . He is best at the spoiling attack; his forte is disruption; he is too impulsive for a set-piece battle. He will do his level best to 'Dunkirk' us."

➣ *Montgomery on Rommel's plans for Normandy*

A Polish prisoner in German uniform near a bunker after the landings.
NATIONAL ARCHIVES

Unable to decide, and always preferring to use bureaucratic in-fighting to bolster his own authority, Hitler split the difference, to the detriment of both Rommel's and Rundstedt's visions. Rommel was given control of three panzer divisions, while four would be kept in reserve closer to Paris (with another three kept in southern France). Hitler would decide, or at least have to approve, when to release and where to move the panzers.

And so the Germans had a defensive network which few top commanders believed would halt the invasion for very long, commanders who did not agree on how best to defeat that invasion, and more than 800,000 troops (with perhaps 40,000 on the beaches) of varying quality ready to meet the Allies—who were prepared to land more than 150,000 on the first day and tens of thousands a day thereafter. If the Germans could deny the Allies a beachhead, they stood a chance of defeating the invasion when it came.

It would not come on June 5 as planned; the weather was not promising. Allied meteorologists forecast just enough of a break for the following day. Early on the morning of the fifth, Eisenhower finalized June 6 as D-Day: "OK, let's go."

D-DAY

On the night of June 5, 1944, aircraft engines thrummed to life at airfields around England. Gear-laden, face-painted men climbed aboard. Gliders were hooked to their tugs. Planes lifted into the night, bound for the English Channel and beyond. Some would drop bombs into Normandy; others would drop men. The invasion was on.

Earlier in the evening, Dwight Eisenhower visited the 101st Airborne Division before paratroopers set off for Normandy. After giving the green light that morning, the Supreme Commander had spent the day smoking by the pack, drinking coffee by the pot, and trying to conceal his nervousness. In his wallet he carried a handwritten draft of a message to be sent out if the operation failed: he intended to take full responsibility. At the airfields, Ike chatted with the airborne soldiers, boosting their morale—and his as well. He remained long enough to watch the planes take off.

General Eisenhower speaks to paratroopers of the 101st Airborne before their D-Day drops.
NATIONAL ARCHIVES

Paratroopers prepare to board planes. Unit insignia have been removed by censors, but these are men of the 101st.
NATIONAL ARCHIVES

Screaming Eagles aboard a C-47. It appears that the second paratrooper from the right is holding a copy of Eisenhower's order of the day.
NATIONAL ARCHIVES

For years the invasion had been an idea. For months it had been a plan in the minds of generals. Now the invasion was a reality. Now its fate, and possibly the outcome of the war, rested largely in the hands of the men in the sky and the men on the water.

The Airborne Landings

The British jumped first. In the eastern sector of the invasion zone behind Sword Beach, British gliders descended into Normandy minutes after midnight. With impressive precision, the gliders landed near the objectives of Operation Deadstick: the bridges over the Orne River and the Caen Canal at the town of Bénouville, about halfway between the city of Caen and the English Channel. The bridges carried the main road from Sword Beach toward Paris—a road essential to the forward progress of the invasion and to any German effort to get reinforcements to the beaches. Capturing the bridges intact was the mission of a company of 180 men of the British 6th Airborne Division. It took the paratroopers fifteen minutes to seize them. Lt. Den Brotheridge became the first Allied soldier killed on D-Day. The canal bridge would enter history as Pegasus Bridge in honor of the British airborne troops.

The Message Eisenhower Never Delivered

On the night of June 5, General Eisenhower drafted the message he intended to deliver if the invasion failed:

Our landings in the Cherbourg-Havre area have failed to gain a satisfactory foothold and I have withdrawn the troops. My decision to attack at this time and place was based upon the best information available. The troops, the air and the Navy did all that bravery and devotion to duty could do. If any blame or fault attaches to the attempt it is mine alone. ■

About twenty minutes later, the main force of the 6th Airborne began to land in scattered fashion, thanks to clouds, wind, pilot error, and German antiaircraft fire. Lone paratroopers and small groups sought each other in the area east and northeast of Caen, gradually forming larger groups that could tackle the division's objectives. With only 150 of its 600 men, a battalion assaulted the German gun battery at Merville, a position that threatened Sword Beach. Suffering 50

Eisenhower's Order of the Day, June 6, 1944

Soldiers, Sailors and Airmen of the Allied Expeditionary Force!

You are about to embark upon the Great Crusade, toward which we have striven these many months. The eyes of the world are upon you. The hopes and prayers of liberty-loving people everywhere march with you. In company with our brave Allies and brothers-in-arms on other Fronts, you will bring about the destruction of the German war machine, the elimination of Nazi tyranny over the oppressed peoples of Europe, and security for ourselves in a free world.

Your task will not be an easy one. Your enemy is well trained, well equipped and battle hardened. He will fight savagely.

But this is the year 1944! Much has happened since the Nazi triumphs of 1940–41. The United Nations have inflicted upon the Germans great defeats, in open battle, man-to-man. Our air offensive has seriously reduced their strength in the air and their capacity to wage war on the ground.

Our Home Fronts have given us a superiority in weapons and munitions of war, and placed at our disposal great reserves of trained fighting men. The tide has turned! The free men of the world marching together to Victory!

I have full confidence in your devotion to duty and skill in battle. We will accept nothing less than full Victory!

Good Luck! And let us all beseech the blessing of Almighty God upon this great and noble undertaking. ■

percent casualties, the paratroopers neutralized the battery on schedule. Farther to the east, airborne soldiers destroyed bridges over the Dives River. More than 8,000 British and Canadian troops landed via parachute and glider that morning; 800 were killed or wounded.

It was like a swarm of maddened bees."

➤ *German soldier observing the drops*

Fifty miles to the west at the eastern base of the Cotentin Peninsula, American paratroopers were experiencing similar problems with dispersed drops. In Mission Albany at 1:30 a.m., the Screaming

Eagles of Maxwell Taylor's 101st Airborne Division—nearly 7,000 paratroopers—dropped behind Utah Beach to secure the beach exits for the infantry, destroy bridges, and neutralize German coastal batteries. Scattered around three drop zones north of Carentan and east of Ste. Mère Église in an area of more than twenty square miles, pockets of paratroopers roamed the marshes and hedgerows, clicking their metal "crickets"—handheld toy clickers—to identify themselves and congealing into groups large enough to execute their missions. Most of D-Day for the 101st was spent regrouping and fighting a series of small-unit clashes, but they did achieve their primary objective of helping to secure the beach exits.

Following the 101st by about an hour, waves of the 82nd Airborne Division—veterans of combat jumps in Sicily and Italy, commanded by Matthew Ridgway—began landing west of the crossroads town Ste. Mère Église, which the All Americans were to capture along with bridges over the Merderet River. Scattered drops plagued much of the 82nd, but a more accurate drop in the zone northwest of Ste. Mère Église enabled the paratroopers to take the important town within a couple of hours. The going was tougher farther to the west along the Merderet,

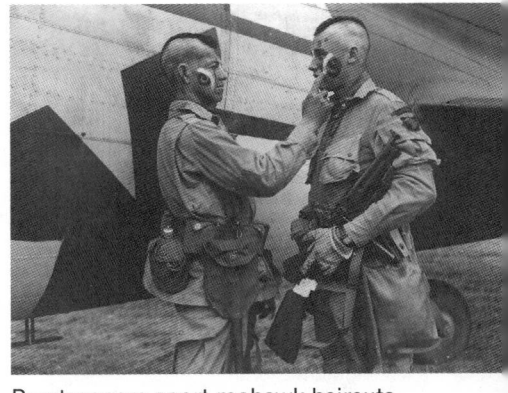

Paratroopers sport mohawk haircuts and warpaint for the invasion. These soldiers are demolitions men, part of a unit of the 101st Airborne calling themselves the Filthy Thirteen.
NATIONAL ARCHIVES

where groups of Americans were attempting without success to seize bridges, including one at La Fière, where fighting would rage for days after D-Day.

D amn, I just cracked the Atlantic Wall."
➤ *American paratrooper*

The Allies had dropped in more than 20,000 paratroopers on the eastern and western flanks of the invasion zone in the early-morning hours of June 6. The results were mixed. Various factors had contributed to the scattering of airborne soldiers across both the American and British sectors, and paratroopers spent valuable time regrouping and making under-manned attempts to achieve their objectives, which was somewhat more successful behind Sword Beach than behind Utah Beach. In both cases, the dispersed drops had caused confusion among the Germans, who, confronting scores of small enemy forces instead of a few large ones, were left guessing about where the main effort might come and whether this was the main effort at all.

Glider reinforcements arrive behind Utah Beach. NATIONAL ARCHIVES

C-47s towing gliders fly over Utah Beach with reinforcements for the airborne divisions. NATIONAL ARCHIVES

A Horsa glider at rest in a field. NATIONAL ARCHIVES

Above: A glider with its tail removed for unloading vehicles. Note the ramps.
NATIONAL ARCHIVES

Below: A glider crash in the 101st Airborne's zone, with eight dead soldiers covered by a parachute. NATIONAL ARCHIVES

The streets of Ste. Mère Église, a vital town seized by the 82nd Airborne on D-Day. NATIONAL ARCHIVES

Right: A paratrooper chats with a French woman and girl in Ste. Mère Église. NATIONAL ARCHIVES

Below: The 82nd Airborne conducts operations in the vicinity of Saint-Marcouf. NATIONAL ARCHIVES

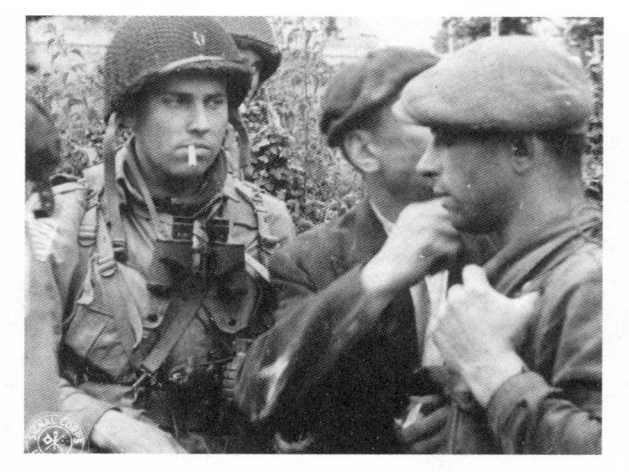

The 82nd Airborne conducts operations in the vicinity of Saint-Marcouf.
NATIONAL ARCHIVES

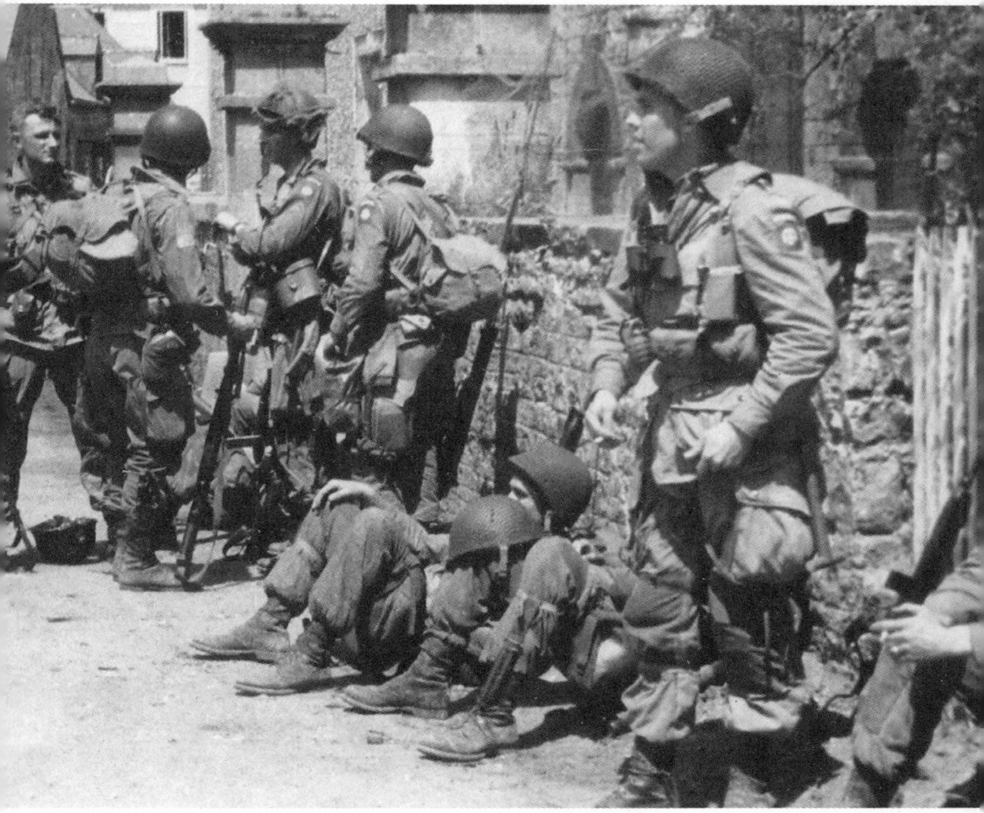

Amphibious Landings

As the planes and gliders flew across the English Channel that night, thousands of ships floated in the water below: battleships, cruisers, destroyers, escorts, transports, monitors, torpedo boats, patrol boats, minesweepers, landing ships and landing craft, barges—an armada of nearly 7,000 vessels and more than 150,000 naval personnel. Few who witnessed it would ever forget the sight. Commanded by Bertram Ramsey of the Royal Navy, the invasion fleet was divided into a Western Task Force for the American sector and an Eastern Task Force for the British-Canadian sector. Since midnight, Allied aircraft had pummeled targets in Normandy and beyond. Now, forty-five minutes before the landings, the warships opened fire on the beaches in a thundering bombardment.

My God, it's the invasion."

➤ *German soldier looking out at the English Channel*

The fleet carried the 150,000 men who would fight on the beaches this day, wave after wave. They had been waiting aboard ships for hours, in many cases for days. Seasick, nervous, excited, scared, gung-ho, talkative, silent, cold, wet: whatever they felt, their moment had arrived.

Landing craft approach Omaha Beach. NATIONAL ARCHIVES

Omaha Beach

The Omaha Beach sector stretched five miles from, roughly, Vierville-sur-Mer in the west to Ste. Honorine in the east. Its natural terrain was imposing. A shingle beach of stones and pebbles sloped upward from the water, terminating in a seawall, which was followed by a flat area of sand extending 200 yards to the foot of steep bluffs. Exits from the beach were via five draws that cut through the bluffs. To these natural defenses, the Germans added lines of obstacles starting in the surf and continuing on the beach. On the bluffs, concentrated at the draws, they built a series of strongpoints with minefields in between. An entire German division, the 352nd, was stationed in the area.

Tasked with attacking this most formidable of the five D-Day beaches were the American 1st and 29th Infantry Divisions. The 1st, the fabled Big Red One, was perhaps the most veteran unit in the U.S. Army at the time, having landed in North Africa in Operation Torch in November 1942, after which it fought at Kasserine Pass and in Tunisia before moving on to Sicily, where the division saw brutal combat in the island's mountains. Known as the Blue and Gray because it drew its men from states that contributed units to North and South in the Civil War (Maryland and Virginia most significantly, but also Kentucky and North Carolina), the 29th was a National Guard division that had yet to see combat in World War II.

The Channel was packed with activity on June 6. Here PT boats sail while B-17s fly above. U.S. NAVY

A chaplain conducts mass for sailors and soldiers aboard a naval vessel in the English Channel. U.S. NAVY

President Roosevelt's D-Day Radio Prayer

Almighty God: Our sons, pride of our nation, this day have set upon a mighty endeavor, a struggle to preserve our Republic, our religion, and our civilization, and to set free a suffering humanity.

Lead them straight and true; give strength to their arms, stoutness to their hearts, steadfastness in their faith.

They will need Thy blessings. Their road will be long and hard. For the enemy is strong. He may hurl back our forces. Success may not come with rushing speed, but we shall return again and again; and we know that by Thy grace, and by the righteousness of our cause, our sons will triumph.

They will be sore tried, by night and by day, without rest—until the victory is won. The darkness will be rent by noise and flame. Men's souls will be shaken with the violences of war.

For these men are lately drawn from the ways of peace. They fight not for the lust of conquest. They fight to end conquest. They fight to liberate. They fight to let justice arise, and tolerance and goodwill among all Thy people. They yearn but for the end of battle, for their return to the haven of home.

Some will never return. Embrace these, Father, and receive them, Thy heroic servants, into Thy kingdom...■

"They're murdering us here! Let's move inland and get murdered!"

➤ *Col. Charles Canham,*
U.S. 29th Infantry Division,
at Omaha Beach

The first wave of infantry came in at 6:30 a.m., a regimental combat team from the 29th on the western side of the beach and a regimental combat team from the 1st on the eastern side. Most of the landing craft hit sandbars and had to unload as far as 300 feet from shore, forcing the gear-heavy

soldiers to swim and wade the rest of the way in. Many drowned. Craft drifted eastward, away from their designated landing zones, and deposited men on unfamiliar beach. Wherever they landed, the troops met fire—small arms, mortars, machine guns, and more—from German positions shooting down

Top left: An LCVP (landing craft, vehicle, personnel) smokes during its run to the beach after a bullet struck a grenade. NATIONAL ARCHIVES
Bottom left: LCI (landing craft, infantry) with barrage balloons above.
NATIONAL ARCHIVES
Above: Troops make the final approach to Omaha on an LCVP. NATIONAL ARCHIVES

Above: LCIs en route to Omaha. NATIONAL ARCHIVES

Left: A landing craft off a smoking Omaha Beach. NATIONAL ARCHIVES

on them from above. In the most hellish areas, Germans created a murderous crossfire that ripped at and across the invaders. The aerial and naval bombardments had done little to mute the batteries and machine-gun nests. Soldiers huddled behind German obstacles, behind the seawall, behind dunes, behind whatever tanks were able to make it ashore—behind any protection available. Casualties in some units ran above 50 percent within minutes. The Channel churned red. Heightening the confusion, some units were left without

Landing craft unload.
NATIONAL ARCHIVES

Troops make the final
approach to Omaha on
an LCVP. NATIONAL ARCHIVES

Vessels, vehicles, and
men face the bluffs of
Omaha. NATIONAL ARCHIVES

D-DAY

American Order of Battle, June 6, 1944

SHAEF (Eisenhower)

21st Army Group (Montgomery)

U.S. First Army (Bradley)
  V Corps (Gerow)
    1st Infantry Division
    29th Infantry Division
    Provisional Engineer
      Special Brigade
    Provisional Ranger Group
  VII Corps (Collins)
    4th Infantry Division
    82nd Airborne Division
    90th Infantry Division
    101st Airborne Division
    1st Engineer Special
      Brigade

clear leadership when company commanders and platoon leaders fell, many before even clearing the waterline. Under such conditions it was difficult, if not impossible, for the first wave to carry out offensive operations on Omaha.

A vessel of soldiers nears the beaches. Note the coverings over their rifles.

NATIONAL ARCHIVES

In one of the most famous photographs of D-Day—titled *Into the Jaws of Death*—soldiers of the 1st Infantry Division wade ashore. Note how the bluffs commanded the obstacle-strewn beach. FRANKLIN D. ROOSEVELT PRESIDENTIAL LIBRARY AND MUSEUM

This photograph, taken in calmer hours after D-Day, shows the obstacles the Germans placed on the beaches. The giant "jacks" are hedgehogs, and the seaward-angled poles were sometimes called "Rommel's asparagus." Both, as well as the ramps (angled inland), were often topped with mines. Note as well the beached vehicles, including, in the foreground, a Sherman tank equipped with deep-wading gear. NATIONAL ARCHIVES

More troops unload at Omaha.
NATIONAL ARCHIVES

Aerial view of Omaha.

Right, below:
Engineers arrive.

Above: Infantrymen wade ashore. NATIONAL ARCHIVES

Right: Rescuing the survivors of a sunken landing craft (possibly a few days after D-Day). NATIONAL ARCHIVES

Providing medical assistance to the survivors of a sunken landing craft (possibly a few days after D-Day).
NATIONAL ARCHIVES

Wounded 1st Infantry Division soldiers.
NATIONAL ARCHIVES

A medic of the 1st Infantry Division provides aid to the wounded along the beach.
NATIONAL ARCHIVES

A landing craft evacuates
the wounded.
NATIONAL ARCHIVES

D-DAY

Left: A naval shore fire control party operates its equipment, an SCR-284 on the left (with crank generator) and an SCR-586 handie-talkie on the right.
NATIONAL ARCHIVES

Below: Many German prisoners taken in Normandy turned out to be POWs whom the Germans shipped from the Eastern Front and pressed into menial military service.
NATIONAL ARCHIVES

The second wave followed at 7:00. The situation was much the same for this larger force, which had to confront hidden obstacles now that the tide was coming in as well as the paralyzed vessels and vehicles of the first wave. But the weight of men was beginning to tell as pockets of troops grew in the more protected parts of the beach.

One such area was on the eastern side of the 29th's sector, where smoke from grass fires on the bluffs provided cover and special teams were able to blast a gap through the obstacle belt. Here elements of the 29th, under the firm hand of the division's assistant commander, Norman "Dutch" Cota, were joined by a battalion of Rangers

"The pride of our nation."
NATIONAL ARCHIVES

(redirected from Pointe du Hoc). Toward 8:00, Cota led a group up over the bluffs rather than through the heavily defended beach exits. They were followed over the next hour by hundreds more men who worked their way inland to attack German positions from the rear and, around 11:00, take the village of Vierville. Farther to the east, in the 1st Division's sector, similar progress was being made.

Well, then, goddammit, Rangers, lead the way!"

➤ *Gen. Norman Cota*
on Omaha

Reinforcements arrived late morning, often delayed by traffic jams as landing craft jostled for space to disembark. On the beaches, engineers worked hard under fire to clear more obstacles while infantry-men fought to neutralize German strongpoints so that more troops, as well as tanks and other vehicles, could move inland via the draws. Meanwhile, the groups that had been able to penetrate beyond the bluffs were fighting isolated battles and skirmishes for control of the coastal road and the villages located along it.

"They are digging in on Omaha Beach with their fingernails."
➤ *Gen. Omar Bradley*

By the end of the day and at a cost of more than 2,000 casualties, the Americans had gained a tenuous toehold a mile to a mile and a half deep along a perforated line from Vierville to Le Garde Hameau, far short of the planned five-mile-deep penetration. The Germans still con-trolled parts of the road as well as the village of Colleville, preventing a linkup with the British to the east, let alone with distant Utah Beach.

Soon after D-Day, a steady stream of men, vehicles, and equipment was passing through Omaha.
NATIONAL ARCHIVES

Brig. Gen. Theodore Roosevelt Jr., assistant commander of the 4th Infantry Division.

Added relatively late in the planning for Operation Overlord, Utah Beach was located at the marshy eastern base of the Cotentin Peninsula and separated from the other invasion beaches by the estuary of the Vire River. Utah would provide the Allies with a springboard for cutting off the Cotentin and capturing the port of Cherbourg at the peninsula's northern end.

The U.S. 4th Infantry Division was assigned the amphibious landing at Utah. Not yet tested in combat but thoroughly trained, the 4th was led by Raymond Barton, who was eclipsed by his vigorous assistant commander, Theodore Roosevelt Jr. Not only was he the son of the twenty-sixth president; he was also a decorated veteran of World War I, helped found the American Legion, and served as assistant secretary of the navy, governor of Puerto Rico, and governor-general of the Philippines, as well as vice president of Doubleday Books. In North Africa, he commanded a regiment before becoming assistant commander of the 1st Infantry Division, a role he continued in the Sicily campaign. Now with the 4th, Roosevelt asked to go in with the first wave of assault troops on D-Day. The fifty-six-year-old general would be the oldest soldier

D-Day Medal of Honor Citations: Theodore Roosevelt Jr.

Rank and organization: Brigadier General, U.S. Army. Place and date: Normandy invasion, 6 June 1944. Entered service at: Oyster Bay, N.Y. Birth: Oyster Bay, N.Y. G.O. No.: 77, 28 September 1944. Citation: for gallantry and intrepidity at the risk of his life above and beyond the call of duty on 6 June 1944, in France. After 2 verbal requests to accompany the leading assault elements in the Normandy invasion had been denied, Brig. Gen. Roosevelt's written request for this mission was approved and he landed with the first wave of the forces assaulting the enemy-held beaches. He repeatedly led groups from the beach, over the seawall and established them inland. His valor, courage, and presence in the very front of the attack and his complete unconcern at being under heavy fire inspired the troops to heights of enthusiasm and self-sacrifice. Although the enemy had the beach under constant direct fire, Brig. Gen. Roosevelt moved from one locality to another, rallying men around him, directed and personally led them against the enemy. Under his seasoned, precise, calm, and unfaltering leadership, assault troops reduced beach strong points and rapidly moved inland with minimum casualties. He thus contributed substantially to the successful establishment of the beachhead in France. ∎

to land on June 6. (His son landed with the first wave at Omaha Beach.)

We'll start the war from right here!"
➤ *Gen. Theodore Roosevelt Jr. on Utah*

At 6:30 a.m., infantrymen of the 4th began wading ashore at Utah. Strong currents had pushed the landing craft more than a mile south of their planned zone—fortuitously, to an area the Germans had not fortified as strongly and one in which the pre-landing bombardment had damaged the primary defensive strongpoint. Conducting his own reconnaissance, Roosevelt decided this was a better zone and sent back word for the remaining landing craft to unload there. Wave after wave arrived. Within an hour or two, the beach was secured, and engineers started to clear mines and obstacles while the infantry moved inland to secure the causeways off the beach and through flooded farmland to link up with groups of paratroopers from the 82nd and 101st Airborne.

On D-Day, the 4th got more than 20,000 men ashore and lost about 200 casualties. In part because it landed farther south than planned, the division did not achieve all of its objectives, but it had secured the beachhead and in concert with the paratroopers had driven west to the Merderet River and south to the Douve River, nearly on the doorstep of Carentan.

Left: The USS *Nevada* bombarding German positions near Utah Beach. NATIONAL ARCHIVES

Right: A convoy of landing craft en route to Utah. NATIONAL ARCHIVES

A weapons carrier is launched from a landing craft toward the beach. NATIONAL ARCHIVES

D-DAY

Sailors aboard an LCI fire an Oerlikon 20-millimeter cannon in support of the landings at Utah. NATIONAL ARCHIVES

Above and below: Infantrymen splashing ashore at Utah. NATIONAL ARCHIVES

More men come in.
NATIONAL ARCHIVES

Soldiers climb over the
seawall at Utah Beach.
U.S. NAVY

The 4th Infantry Division
moves inland. The soldier
at left is carrying a Model
1919 Browning machine
gun. NATIONAL ARCHIVES

Soldiers inspect the 210-millimeter gun at the Crisbecq battery near Utah Beach. It was a thorn in the side of the U.S. Army and Navy until its capture on June 12.
NATIONAL ARCHIVES

Prisoners of war on Utah Beach. NATIONAL ARCHIVES

Between Omaha and Utah Beaches, a hundred-foot cliff jutted into the sea. The Germans had fortified this commanding position with 155-millimeter guns in concrete casemates, four of which (out of a planned six) had been completed by the spring of 1944. These massive guns could wreak havoc on the landings at Utah and Omaha. They had to be captured.

That task fell to three companies of the 2nd Ranger Battalion under Lt. Col. James Rudder. Scheduled to land roughly ten minutes after the first wave landed at Omaha, the assault force was delayed more than half an hour by strong currents and navigational problems. (The delay meant that a signal flare for the follow-on 5th Rangers did not go up in time, so that group diverted to Omaha, where it played a pivotal role.) By 7:30, less than half an hour after landing, the Rangers had worked their way up the cliff with ropes, ladders, and their bare hands. At the top, they discovered empty gun casemates: the Germans had removed the guns after being

An infantryman on the move with a Model 1917 Browning machine gun.
NATIONAL ARCHIVES

The Boys of Pointe du Hoc

The story of the Rangers at Pointe du Hoc captivated the world decades after D-Day as President Ronald Reagan marked the fortieth anniversary:

We stand on a lonely, windswept point on the northern shore of France. The air is soft, but 40 years ago at this moment, the air was dense with smoke and the cries of men, and the air was filled with the crack of rifle fire and the roar of cannon. At dawn, on the morning of the 6th of June, 1944, 225 Rangers jumped off the British landing craft and ran to the bottom of these cliffs. Their mission was one of the most difficult and daring of the invasion: to climb these sheer and desolate cliffs and take out the enemy guns. The Allies had been told that some of the mightiest of these guns were here and they would be trained on the beaches to stop the Allied advance.

The Rangers looked up and saw the enemy soldiers—at the edge of the cliffs shooting down at them with machine guns and throwing grenades.

And the American Rangers began to climb. They shot rope ladders over the face of these cliffs and began to pull themselves up. When one Ranger fell, another would take his place. When one rope was cut, a Ranger would grab another and begin his climb again. They climbed, shot back, and held their footing. Soon, one by one, the Rangers pulled themselves over the top, and in seizing the firm land at the top of these cliffs, they began to seize back the continent of Europe. Two hundred and twenty-five came here. After 2 days of fighting, only 90 could still bear arms.

Behind me is a memorial that symbolizes the Ranger daggers that were thrust into the top of these cliffs. And before me are the men who put them there.

These are the boys of Pointe du Hoc. These are the men who took the cliffs. These are the champions who helped free a continent. These are the heroes who helped end a war. ■

bombarded in April. The Rangers quickly found the guns less than half a mile beyond Pointe du Hoc and destroyed them. They had accomplished their mission, but remained isolated and had to fight off German counterattacks for the rest of the day and into the night. Casualties in Rudder's three companies exceeded 50 percent.

D-Day Medal of Honor Citations: Carlton W. Barrett

Rank and organization: Private, U.S. Army, 18th Infantry, 1st Infantry Division. Place and date: Near St. Laurent-sur-Mer, France, 6 June 1944. Entered service at: Albany, N.Y. Birth: Fulton, N.Y. G.O. No.: 78, 2 October 1944. Citation: For gallantry and intrepidity at the risk of his life above and beyond the call of duty on 6 June 1944, in the vicinity of St. Laurent-sur-Mer, France. On the morning of D-Day Pvt. Barrett, landing in the face of extremely heavy enemy fire, was forced to wade ashore through neck-deep water. Disregarding the personal danger, he returned to the surf again and again to assist his floundering comrades and save them from drowning. Refusing to remain pinned down by the intense barrage of small-arms and mortar fire poured at the landing points, Pvt. Barrett, working with fierce determination, saved many lives by carrying casualties to an evacuation boat lying offshore. In addition to his assigned mission as guide, he carried dispatches the length of the fire-swept beach; he assisted the wounded; he calmed the shocked; he arose as a leader in the stress of the occasion. His coolness and his dauntless daring courage while constantly risking his life during a period of many hours had an inestimable effect on his comrades and is in keeping with the highest traditions of the U.S. Army. ■

D-Day Medal of Honor Citations: Jimmie W. Monteith Jr.

Rank and organization: First Lieutenant, U.S. Army, 16th Infantry, 1st Infantry Division. Place and date: Near Colleville-sur-Mer, France, 6 June 1944. Entered service at: Richmond, Va. Born: 1 July 1917, Low Moor, Va. G.O. No.: 20, 29 March 1945. Citation: For conspicuous gallantry and intrepidity above and beyond the call of duty on 6 June 1944, near Colleville-sur-Mer, France. 1st Lt. Monteith landed with the initial assault waves on the coast of France under heavy enemy fire. Without regard to his own personal safety he continually moved up and down the beach reorganizing men for further assault. He then led the assault over a narrow protective ledge and across the flat, exposed terrain to the comparative safety of a cliff. Retracing his steps across the field to the beach, he moved over to where 2 tanks were buttoned up and blind under violent enemy artillery and machinegun fire. Completely exposed to the intense fire, 1st Lt. Monteith led the tanks on foot through a minefield and into firing positions. Under his direction several enemy positions were destroyed. He then rejoined his company and under his leadership his men captured an advantageous position on the hill. Supervising the defense of his newly won position against repeated vicious counterattacks, he continued to ignore his own personal safety, repeatedly crossing the 200 or 300 yards of open terrain under heavy fire to strengthen links in his defensive chain. When the enemy succeeded in completely surrounding 1st Lt. Monteith and his unit and while leading the fight out of the situation, 1st Lt. Monteith was killed by enemy fire. The courage, gallantry, and intrepid leadership displayed by 1st Lt. Monteith is worthy of emulation. ∎

D-Day Medal of Honor Citations: John J. Pinder Jr.

Rank and organization: Technician Fifth Grade, U.S. Army, 16th Infantry, 1st Infantry Division. Place and date: Near Colleville-sur-Mer, France, 6 June 1944. Entered service at: Burgettstown, Pa. Birth: McKees Rocks, Pa. G.O. No.: 1, 4 January 1945. Citation: For conspicuous gallantry and intrepidity above and beyond the call of duty on 6 June 1944, near Colleville-sur-Mer, France. On D-Day, Technician 5th Grade Pinder landed on the coast 100 yards off shore under devastating enemy machinegun and artillery fire which caused severe casualties among the boatload. Carrying a vitally important radio, he struggled towards shore in waist-deep water. Only a few yards from his craft he was hit by enemy fire and was gravely wounded. Technician 5th Grade Pinder never stopped. He made shore and delivered the radio. Refusing to take cover afforded, or to accept medical attention for his wounds, Technician 5th Grade Pinder, though terribly weakened by loss of blood and in fierce pain, on 3 occasions went into the fire-swept surf to salvage communication equipment. He recovered many vital parts and equipment, including another workable radio. On the 3rd trip he was again hit, suffering machinegun bullet wounds in the legs. Still this valiant soldier would not stop for rest or medical attention. Remaining exposed to heavy enemy fire, growing steadily weaker, he aided in establishing the vital radio communication on the beach. While so engaged this dauntless soldier was hit for the third time and killed. The indomitable courage and personal bravery of Technician 5th Grade Pinder was a magnificent inspiration to the men with whom he served. ∎

A soldier communicates via an SCR-300 radio. NATIONAL ARCHIVES

Gold, Juno, and Sword

The British and Canadian beaches began approximately eight miles to the east of Omaha Beach and stretched from Port-en-Bessin in the west to the mouth of the Orne River in the east. At Gold, the British 50th Infantry Division would land with the objectives of capturing Arromanches and Bayeux and connecting with the Americans at Omaha. At Juno, the Canadian 3rd Infantry Division was to land and drive inland to cut the Caen–Bayeux road and railroad and take the airfield west of Caen. At Sword, the British 3rd Infantry Division was tasked with capturing Caen itself, some ten miles from the beaches.

The 50th (Northumbrian) Division was as battle-tested as they come. After fighting in the Battle of France and evacuating at Dunkirk in 1940, the division shipped out to the Mediterranean the following year, participated in the two-year seesaw of battles (including Second Alamein) that defeated the Axis in Africa, and then invaded Sicily before returning home to prepare for D-Day. New to battle, the Canadian 3rd Infantry Division had been stationed in the United Kingdom since 1941. Its regiments highlighted the proud heritage of Canada: The Royal Winnipeg Rifles, The Queen's Own Rifles of Canada, Le Régiment de La Chaudière, and the Stormont, Dundas, and Glengarry Highlanders, among others. The British 3rd Division boasted a lineage dating to its formation by the Duke of Wellington and a battle history including Waterloo, the Crimean War, the Boer War, and World War I, where beaches were accompanied by the so-called "Hobart's Funnies" of the 79th Armoured Division. These vehicles were modified tanks suited for various engineering purposes, including flamethrower tanks for clearing bunkers, assault vehicles (AVREs) that blasted obstacles with high-explosive projectiles, and the Crab, a tank that spun chains in front of it to detonate mines. (The U.S. Army opted not to use the Funnies, a decision some have argued contributed to the difficulties on Omaha Beach.)

A re we dreaming? Is it all really true? We are at last liberated."

➤ *French woman near Gold Beach*

The western prong of the Gold Beach assault ran into heavy fire from a German strongpoint at Le Hamel that had not been destroyed by the pre-landing bombardment as planned. The strongpoint, which boasted a powerful 75-millimeter gun, unleashed terrible enfilading fire down the beach. Slowing British progress even further, the Germans had laid a particularly effective band of obstacles near the gun emplacement and withdrew into fortified houses nearby. The men of the 50th would have to fight house to house before taking out the strongpoint. The big gun was not

it became known as the Iron Division. It had fought with distinction in France in 1940 but had not seen combat since then.

Because the tides were different in this zone, the British-Canadian landings began about an hour after the landings at the American beaches. The British 3rd Infantry Division landed at Sword around 7:30, with the 50th Division hitting Gold at approximately the same time. The Canadian 3rd Division waded onto Juno twenty minutes later. The infantrymen on these

General Montgomery's Order of the Day, June 6, 1944

The time has come to deal the enemy a terrific blow in Western Europe. The blow will be struck by the combined sea, land and air forces of the Allies—together constituting one great Allied team under the supreme command of General Eisenhower. On the eve of this great adventure, I send my best wishes to every soldier in the Allied team. To us is given the honor of striking a blow for freedom which will live in history, and in the better days that lie ahead, men will speak with pride of our doings. We have a great and a righteous cause.

Let us pray that "The Lord Mighty in Battle" will go forth with our armies and that His special providence will aid us in the struggle. I want every soldier to know that I have complete confidence in the successful outcome of the operations that we are now about to begin. With stout hearts, and with enthusiasm for the contest, let us go forward to victory.

And as we enter the battle let us recall the words of a famous soldier spoken many years ago:

> He either fears his fate too much,
> Or his deserts are small,
> Who dares not put it to the touch
> To win or lose it all.

Good luck to each one of you. And good hunting on the mainland of Europe. ■

---

silenced until late afternoon, after which troops advanced on Arromanches to the west. On the eastern side of Gold, a German 88-millimeter gun at La Rivière threatened to unleash the same fury on the British invaders, but a special engineering unit cleared a path to the gun and scored a direct hit in the very early stages of the landings.

Once the guns were neutralized, forces began working inland, southwest toward the Caen–Bayeux road and Bayeux itself. They were joined by 47 Royal Marine Commando, which came ashore about an hour after the initial landing, and turned west toward Port-en-Bessin, a strategically important Channel town whose seizure would help effect the link-up with Omaha Beach and provide the location for a planned Allied fuel depot. At the end of the day, the commandos dug in on an elevation south of Port-en-Bessin, ready to launch an attack the next day.

At Gold, the British landed 25,000 men at a cost of 1,000 casualties. They fell somewhat short of achieving all their objectives, but they were poised to gain most of them in the next day or two.

East of Gold, at Juno Beach, the Germans greeted the Canadians with heavy fire from 88-millimeter and 75-millimeter guns as well as machine guns. The preliminary bombardment had not been effective here, where casualties in some of the assault companies ran as high as 50 percent. The Canadians persevered and broke through German defenses, only to run into a series of fortified villages that, protected by mortars and snipers, blocked the way to the Caen–Bayeux road and the Carpiquet Airfield.

To see tanks coming out of the water shook them rigid."

➤ *Canadian soldier on the Germans at Juno*

By day's end, the Canadians landed 21,000 men and took casualties of just under 1,000. Though they did not secure the road or the airfield, they made the most gains of any of the five Allied beaches—and achieved the important linkup with the British at Gold. Making contact

with Sword would prove more difficult.

At Sword, the far eastern beach of the invasion, the British encountered a nettlesome band of mines and obstacles, but the engineers, aided by the "Funnies," quickly cleared the beach as well as all but one of the exits. Infantry worked their way inland toward Caen, supported by commandos on their eastern and western flanks.

To the east, the 1st Special Service Brigade was tasked with taking the town of Ouistreham. This unit was led by Simon Fraser, Lord Lovat, a colorful thirty-two-year-old Scottish clan chief. He led one of the few successes in the otherwise disastrous Dieppe raid. His men likened him to Shakespeare's King Henry V; Hitler wanted him captured and killed. The first commando into the water at Sword, Lovat had his personal bagpiper, Bill Millin, play the pipes—against orders forbidding such performances—while the unit waded ashore. Unarmed and wearing a kilt (without undergarments, it is said), Millin did so in one of D-Day's most stirring moments, later immortalized in the film *The Longest Day*. From Ouistreham, the commandos moved south to meet up with British paratroopers at Pegasus Bridge.

Victoria Cross Citation: Stanley Hollis

*O*nly one British-Canadian soldier *was awarded a Victoria Cross on D-Day: Stanley Hollis at Gold Beach. This is his citation:*

In Normandy, France, on 6th June 1944, during the assault on the beaches and the Mont Fleury battery, CSM Hollis's Company Commander noticed that two of the pillboxes had been by-passed and went with CSM Hollis to see that they were clear. When they were 20 yards from the pillbox, a machine gun opened fire from the slit and CSM Hollis instantly rushed straight at the pillbox, firing his Sten gun. He jumped on top of the pillbox, recharged his magazine, threw a grenade in through the door and fired his Sten gun into it, killing two Germans and making the remainder prisoner. He then cleared several Germans from a neighbouring trench. By his action he undoubtedly saved his Company from being fired on heavily from the rear and enabled them to open the main beach exit.

Later the same day in the village of Crepon, the Company encountered a field gun and crew armed with Spandaus at 100 yards range. CSM Hollis was put in command of a party to cover an attack on the gun, but the movement was held up. Seeing this, CSM Hollis pushed right forward to engage the gun with a PIAT from a house at 50 yards range. He was observed by a sniper who fired and grazed his right cheek and at the same moment the gun swung round and fired at point blank range into the house. To avoid the falling masonry CSM Hollis moved his party to an alternative position. Two of the enemy gun crew had by this time been killed and the gun was destroyed shortly afterwards. He later found that two of his men had stayed behind in the house and immediately volunteered to get them out. In full view of the enemy who were continually firing at him, he went forward alone using a Bren gun to distract their attention from the other men. Under cover of his diversion, the two men were able to get back.

Wherever the fighting was heaviest CSM Hollis appeared and, in the course of a magnificent day's work, he displayed the utmost gallantry and on two separate occasions his courage and initiative prevented the enemy from holding up the advance at critical stages. It was largely through his heroism and resource that the Company's objectives were gained and casualties were not heavier, and by his own bravery he saved the lives of many of his men. ∎

G ive us 'Highland Laddie,' man."

➤ *Lord Lovat, ordering up his bagpiper*

The commandos to the west, the 4th Special Service Brigade, met stiff resistance in their efforts to take Lion-sur-Mer and link up with the Canadians at Juno. By late afternoon, a wide gap still separated Sword and Juno. It was here that the Germans made their only major counterattack of the day.

The landings did not completely surprise the Germans, who had been expecting and preparing for an invasion for many months, but the Allies landed at a moment when the Germans were not at all ready to take swift, concerted, coordinated countermeasures. Rommel, Army Group B commander, was in Germany, on leave for his wife's birthday, and would not reach the front until late that night. The Seventh Army's commander and other officers were at war games in Rennes, a hundred miles away. The commander of the 21st Panzer Division, one of the units intended to be used early in any response, was missing —possibly in Paris with his mistress. Hitler, who retained control of the all-important panzer reserves, was asleep, and aides feared waking him. Hitler (once awake) and his staff were slow to recognize that this was *the* invasion and not simply a diversion, and therefore were reluctant to release the reserves.

N ow we have them where we can destroy them."

➤ *Hitler on the invasion*

That left the 21st Panzer Division to strike back against the Allies, which the unit was at last ready to do near 4:00 in the afternoon of D-Day. From positions around Caen, the panzers rolled north. To the east, they attacked toward the British airborne zone around Bénouville; the British quickly stopped them. The main effort came in the gap between Juno and Sword, where the Germans threatened to hit both beaches in the flank and perhaps roll them up. Here the 21st reached the Channel, but overextended, unreinforced, and exposed to air attack, the division could not exploit or even hold its gains. It withdrew to a line around Caen, an objective which the panzer attack had in any event rendered unattainable to the British.

At Sword, though they had not captured Caen as planned, the British had landed more than 25,000 men and suffered not quite 700 casualties.

By the end of June 6, 1944, American, British, and Canadian

Celebrity Participants in D-Day

Yogi Berra, U.S. Navy. The future Yankee Hall of Famer served as a gunner's mate on the USS *Bayfield* and manned the machine guns on a support landing craft a few hundred yards from the beach.

James Doohan, 3rd Canadian Infantry Division. At Juno Beach, Lieutenant Doohan led his men through a minefield, took out two snipers, and was later wounded by friendly fire. He went on to fame as *Star Trek*'s Scotty.

Henry Fonda, U.S. Navy. The actor was a quartermaster on the USS *Satterlee*, which provided naval support at Pointe du Hoc. He later portrayed Theodore Roosevelt Jr. in the D-Day epic *The Longest Day*.

John Ford, U.S. Navy. The Oscar-winning director landed with a camera crew at Omaha Beach.

Alec Guinness, Royal Navy. The future Obi-Wan and Oscar winner for *Bridge on the River Kwai* skippered a British landing craft.

J.D. Salinger, U.S. 4th Infantry Division. The writer landed on Utah Beach carrying, it is reported, draft chapters of *The Catcher in the Rye*.

Jimmy Stewart, U.S. Army Air Force. A decorated combat pilot as well as an Academy Award winner, Stewart served as operations officer of an Eighth Air Force bomb group that made bombing runs on D-Day. ■

---

forces had fallen short of the geographic objectives of Overlord—the best plans often fall apart in the face of the enemy—but succeeded in landing, by air and sea, 150,000 men in Normandy, with fewer casualties than expected, with the painful exception of Omaha Beach. Some sectors remained unsecured. The Germans had potent

reinforcements heading for the beachheads. But D-Day had to be judged a success. General Eisenhower's deliver-in-case-of-failure message could remain in his wallet.

O**verlord is a source of joy to us all."**

➤ *Joseph Stalin to Winston Churchill*

THE
NORMANDY
CAMPAIGN

T he Allies had cracked the Germans' Atlantic Wall and acquired a foothold in Normandy on June 6, but D-Day was only part of Operation Overlord—an essential one to be sure, but only a first step into Western Europe. Next came the great leap through France to Germany's doorstep.

Buildup and Consolidation

First the Allies needed to build up the hundreds of thousands of men and many thousands of tons of equipment required to continue the invasion of Normandy. In the area within 200 miles of the beaches, the Germans outnumbered the Allies by two to one during these early days, a numerical superiority that would hold up until the Allies could open a secure conduit of supplies. Air attacks on roadways, railroads, and German convoys would help stall reinforcements headed for the beaches, but the Allies needed to act swiftly.

The American mulberry at Omaha Beach. NATIONAL ARCHIVES

Men and materiel would be landed directly on the beaches and via artificial harbors code-named "mulberries." Unwilling to attempt an amphibious assault on a port after the abortive 1942 raid at Dieppe, Allied planners knew they would have to rely on the beachhead itself as a conduit for soldiers and supplies. The idea of artificial harbors had originated with Winston Churchill, who proposed the concept during the First World War and suggested it again even before the Dieppe disaster. Developed by British engineers and prefabricated in Britain, mulberries were constructed by sinking old ships ("corncobs") and placing concrete caissons ("phoenixes") to create calm breakwaters; floating piers ("whales") ran to shore from docked ships. On the afternoon of D-Day, the first of the 10,000 men and the first of more than a million tons required to build the two mulberries ("A" in the American sector at Omaha Beach, "B" in the British sector at Gold) were on their way to Normandy. Both were partially operational during the first week and approaching completion at the end of the second week, when a storm wrecked the Omaha mulberry. The Gold Beach harbor—nicknamed "Port Winston," after the prime minister—remained operational for more than six months, until the capture of ports rendered it unnecessary.

A n idea of simple genius."

> *Albert Speer on the mulberries*

Some 325,000 troops had been landed in Normandy by June 10, 500,000 by June 20, and 750,000 by the end of the month. By that time, the Allies were landing nearly 16,000 tons of supplies each day through the mulberries and on the various beaches.

To support this buildup and to be able to advance inland, the Allies needed a single consolidated beachhead. The attack of the German 21st Panzer Division on the afternoon of June 6 had severed

Juno and Sword Beaches, but the British and Canadians linked the two on the seventh. On June 8, Gold and Omaha were joined. Closing the gap between Omaha and Utah proved more difficult and depended on the capture of the town of Carentan, a D-Day objective rendered impossible to achieve because of the scattered parachute drops behind Utah Beach and the difficulties at Omaha. On June 10, the U.S. 101st Airborne Division, now regrouped, launched its attack on Carentan, which was defended by German paratroopers. The town fell after three days, at last giving the Allies a continuous beachhead.

The wrecked mulberry at Omaha after the Channel storm. NATIONAL ARCHIVES

Soldiers and civilians in Ste. Marie du Mont, June 12. NATIONAL ARCHIVES

German prisoners of war.
NATIONAL ARCHIVES

Street fighting in Cherbourg.
NATIONAL ARCHIVES

The Tulle and Oradour-sur-Glane Massacres

The 2nd SS Panzer Division, known as *Das Reich*, had been stationed in France since February 1944. Veterans of punishing fighting on the Eastern Front and thoroughly indoctrinated in Nazi ideology, *Das Reich* had been attempting since May to root out elements of the French Resistance in their sector 250 miles south of Paris.

On D-Day, the Resistance staged an uprising and retreated into Tulle, where *Das Reich* attacked on June 7, taking the town the next day. Reprisals began on the ninth with the arrests of some 5,000 men, the hanging of 99 from balconies and lampposts, and the deportation to Dachau of 149. Reports of torture would come out of Tulle for weeks.

This was only the beginning. Rolling north to greet the Allied invasion, parts of *Das Reich* stopped at Oradour-sur-Glane on June 10 based on reports that a kidnapped German officer was being held nearby. (He may have been at Oradour-sur-*Vayres*, nearly twenty miles away.) The Germans gathered up the men, locked them in barns, gunned them down, doused them in gasoline, and ignited the bodies. The women and children were imprisoned in the church, which the SS men set ablaze, machine-gunning anyone trying to flee the inferno. Unverifiable reports of a ghastly bacchanalia of champagne, accordions, crucifixion, and a baby in an oven circulated. The horrific death toll was 642, including 247 women and 205 children. Oradour-sur-Glane ceased to exist. It remains a ghost town today, preserved virtually as it was after *Das Reich* completed its appalling work. ∎

Cherbourg and the *Bocage*

By June 12, when American paratroopers captured Carentan, the U.S. Army held the southeastern corner of the Cotentin Peninsula and had pushed almost twenty miles south of Omaha Beach, to the edge of the town of Caumont. There the southern drive had paused so that attention could be given to Cherbourg.

Less than a week after the fall of Carentan, U.S. forces under J. Lawton Collins reached the western side of the Cotentin, effectively sealing off the German garrison in Cherbourg. While Eisenhower, Bradley, and Patton were commanding operations in North Africa and Sicily, Collins had been fighting in the Pacific, where his aggressive leadership on Guadalcanal earned him the nickname "Lightning Joe." Now in France, Collins wasted little time before turning north and advancing on Cherbourg with three divisions spread across the peninsula. The English Channel storm that wrecked the Omaha mulberry made the capture of the port urgently necessary. Preceded by a massive aerial attack and supported by naval bombardment, American infantrymen took Cherbourg—where the Germans were ensconced in bunkers and tunnels—in the last week of June. The Germans had mined, booby-trapped, and otherwise demolished the harbor; it would take months to restore it fully, by which time the Allies had captured other ports.

"Sometimes I wish I had George Patton over there."

➤ *Dwight Eisenhower during the June hedgerow battles*

By the end of June, the Americans had secured the Cotentin and captured nearly 40,000 prisoners, but otherwise, their line in Normandy remained little changed. In this early stage of the campaign, resources permitted only one major operation at a time, and the effort to take Cherbourg received priority. Also hindering forward progress, south of Omaha Beach as well as in the Cotentin, was the *bocage* country. This was an area of meadows, pastures, and woods separated by mazes of hedgerows and sunken roads. Hedgerows were mounds of earth as high as three to four feet—sometimes higher—and at least as many feet thick. Most were hundreds of years old, with some dating back to the Romans and Vikings, and were tangled with trees and hedges whose roots grew deep into the embankments. Hedgerows limited mobility and fields of fire, obscured views, and created formidable defensive positions for the Germans. American planners had underestimated the difficulties of this terrain, which were made worse by rainy weather.

The *Bocage* Country

James A. Huston, a young intelligence officer in the U.S. 35th Infantry Division, details the challenges of the peculiar Normandy landscape:

By digging a deep foxhole—a covered one—behind and in these hedgerows, the defender could make himself almost immune from all kinds of small arms or shell fire. But that was not his only, nor his greatest advantage. There was the observation which he denied his attackers but enjoyed himself. He could have his guns zeroed in, put an observer up in a tree and wait. The attacker, on the other hand, usually could not see more than one hedgerow ahead, and could almost never see any enemy activity; and then when he did discover the enemy's presence by suddenly finding himself pinned down by enemy fire, he was too close to employ his own artillery. At the same time, the enemy found that these hedgerows provided him with covered routes for supply and evacuation and withdrawal. There were numerous roads and lanes—always running between hedgerows—leading in all directions. . . . In a hedge-row system of defense the first dike usually was held by only a few men as an outpost line—frequently armed with machine pistols. The second row was likely to be defended more fully; it would have riflemen and machine guns well dug in, with firing slits through the hedgerows. The third, also held with machine guns and rifles, was more thoroughly prepared with extensive tunneling and digging. The entire position was covered by well-coordinated artillery and mortar fire. Snipers, mines, booby traps, filled in the defense pattern. In a heavy attack, men from the first hedgerow tended to withdraw to the second or third and continue the defense. Key positions were those at the corners—near junctions of hedgerows—whence machine guns could cover the entire field in an exchange of fire with a machine gun at the next corner. Above, denying advance to the attacking troops, these automatic weapons would pin them down—fix them on a target where they would become easy prey to the bursting shells of high-angle mortar fire. ∎

(From *Biography of a Battalion*)

Above: Omar Bradley (left) and
J. Lawton Collins. NATIONAL ARCHIVES
Right: The *bocage* country.
NATIONAL ARCHIVES

"The damndest country I've seen."

> ➤ *Omar Bradley on the* bocage

American operations in the *bocage* south of the Cotentin made only slow, bloody progress in early July, trading thousands of casualties for gains of a few miles in the direction of an east–west line through St. Lô. More open ground tantalized U.S. commanders to the south past Avranches—where mobility and maneuver could be restored, where the wide enveloping swing to the east along the Loire River was to take place—but seemed painfully farther away than the fifty miles on the map.

M5A1 Stuart tank. NATIONAL ARCHIVES

THE NORMANDY CAMPAIGN

Caen

The absence of *bocage* in much of the British-Canadian sector allowed more room for maneuver—for the Allies as well as for the Germans, who concentrated their best panzer divisions around the city of Caen, an important roadway junction nine miles from the coast and a gateway to flat, open ground to the south. Planned to be captured on D-Day, the city remained untaken for weeks afterward.

A few days after D-Day, Montgomery launched an operation (code-named Perch) to encircle Caen. After German armor halted an initial attempt west of Caen at Tilly-sur-Seulles, Montgomery tried again farther to the west. At Villers-Bocage on June 13, a brigade of the 7th Armoured Division—the Desert Rats, celebrated veterans of the war in Africa—was ambushed by a German Tiger tank battalion. Weighing more than 50 tons and packing a devastating 88-millimeter punch, the Tiger easily outmatched Allied tanks on paper and in most battlefield situations. In an ambush, with seasoned aces like Michael Wittmann in the turret, the Tigers wreaked havoc at Villers-Bocage. Perch was called off.

Know your explosives: an array of various mines, grenades, and other demolition equipment. NATIONAL ARCHIVES

THE NORMANDY CAMPAIGN

"They went at it like hockey players."

➤ *Canadian corporal at Caen*

Montgomery tried again two weeks later while the Americans were clearing out Cherbourg. Operation Epsom failed to take Caen but managed to get across a river southwest of the city—another step toward Caen's encirclement—and pin down panzer units that the Germans had planned to use in a counterattack to the west. With the Americans bogged down south of the Cotentin and with the British and Canadians slowed at Caen, Montgomery tried to blast into the city on July 7 with a Royal Air Force bombardment of nearly 2,500 tons—a later generation might call it "shock and awe"—followed by a ground assault (Operation Charnwood). The infantry took only the northern part of the leveled and cratered city. It took a further operation (Goodwood) to secure the rest of the city on July 18–20, more than forty days after D-Day.

Breakout

On July 18, elements of the U.S. 29th Infantry Division entered the bombed-out city of St. Lô, led by Gen. Norman Cota, one of the heroes of Omaha Beach. In front of the city's ruined Notre-Dame

Operation Goodwood Order of Battle, July 18, 1944

21st Army Group (Montgomery)

Second Army (Dempsey)
  I Corps (Crocker)
    3rd Infantry Division
    51st Infantry Division
  VIII Corps (O'Connor)
    Guards Armoured Division
    7th Armoured Division
    11th Armoured Division

church, the 29ers deposited the body of Maj. Thomas Howie, who had been killed earlier that day. The 29th and the 35th Infantry Divisions had been slogging their way through the hedgerows around the city for a week and now stood on the verge of achieving their objective—at a cost of 5,000 casualties. The July crawl through the *bocage* had produced 40,000 American wounded and dead. "The Major of St. Lô," draped in a flag atop a pile of ancient stone in "The Capital of Ruins" (as writer Samuel Beckett called the city), testified to the sacrifice—and indeed the waste,

In the Hedgerows near St. Lô

Maj. Glover Johns, a battalion commander in the U.S. 29th Infantry Division, describes a horrifying, but ultimately poignant, moment during his unit's fight toward the Normandy city:

While the major wondered dully what he might do next, he saw a hand come over the nearby hedgerow. It was groping uncertainly, searching for a hold. It found the root of a bush and was followed by a ghastly caricature of a face. The man had been struck by a fragment that had slashed across his nose and both eyes in a great jagged cut from which the blood still flowed. Johns watched in dumb horror as the man pulled himself up on the hedgerow and then fell over on the near side. He rolled several feet beyond the base before he could pull himself together and resume his painful crawling on hands and knees.

Only then did Johns find his voice. "For God's sake, GET that man," he shouted, leaping to his feet.

A runner and a commando got to the soldier first. They laid him gently down next to the hedgerow. The commando tore open a first-aid pouch and gently bandaged the awful wound. It was impossible to tell if the man had lost his eyes. The runner put a handful of sulfa pills into the man's mouth and gave him a canteen of water. The man gagged, swallowed, then lay back limply. In a moment, he started to struggle to his feet. The CO put his hand on the man's shoulder, saying, "Take it easy, son, we'll have a litter squad here for you in a little bit."

The man calmly threw off the restraining hand and struggled to his feet as he said, "That's okay, sir, I can make it and there's a lot of others need the litters more'n I do." ∎

(From *The Clay Pigeons of St. Lô*)

however necessary—of the Allied campaign to liberate Europe.

The battle for St. Lô turned out to be the climax of the *bocage* campaign and opened the way for Operation Cobra, which Gen. Omar Bradley, commander of the U.S. First Army, had started planning a week before the 29th entered

St. Lô. A 1915 graduate of West Point, where he played varsity baseball, Bradley, like his classmate and friend Eisenhower, did not see combat in World War I. His interwar career featured a series of teaching assignments that culminated in command of the Infantry School. After the U.S. entered World

Above: A mine has destroyed a vehicle near St. Lô, July 20. NATIONAL ARCHIVES
Below: Thomas Howie, the Major of St. Lô, at rest in the rubble of the Notre-Dame church. NATIONAL ARCHIVES

Omar Bradley Career Highlights

1893	Born in Missouri
1915	Graduates from West Point (44 of 164)
1915–17	Serves on Mexican border
1918–19	Battalion commander
1919–20	ROTC professor, South Dakota State College
1920–24	Mathematics instructor, West Point
1924–25	Attends Infantry School
1928–29	Attends Command and General Staff School
1929–33	Instructor, Infantry School
1933–34	Army War College
1934–38	Instructor, West Point
1938–41	Assistant secretary, General Staff
1941	Promoted to brigadier general
	Commander, Infantry School
1942	Commander, 82nd Infantry (later Airborne) Division
	Commander, 28th Infantry Division
1943	Advisor to Eisenhower in North Africa
	Deputy corps commander under Patton
	Corps commander in North Africa, then in Sicily
1944	Commands U.S. First Army: D-Day, Normandy
1944–45	Commands U.S. 12th Army Group: Normandy through end of war
1945–47	Leads Veterans Administration
1948–49	U.S. Army Chief of Staff
1949–53	Chairman of the Joint Chiefs of Staff
Sept 1950	Promoted to General of the Army
1970	Consultant for movie *Patton*
1981	Dies in New York City

War II, Bradley briefly commanded two stateside divisions before going to North Africa to serve as Eisenhower's troubleshooter, a deputy corps commander under Patton, and a corps commander in the final stage of the North African campaign and then in Sicily, after which he went to London to participate in Overlord planning and command the First Army. Ernie Pyle christened Bradley "the G.I.'s general" after Eisenhower encouraged the journalist to write about him, but Bradley's modest, plain demeanor—in contrast to Patton (whom Bradley disliked, and vice-versa)—concealed a shrewd operator who could be rigid in his thinking and for whom regular infantrymen had no special affection.

I **want it to be the biggest thing in the world. We want to smash right through."**

> *Omar Bradley on Cobra*

Cobra would be Bradley's masterstroke. Whereas earlier operations in Normandy had unfolded across a broad front, the Cobra plan—devised largely by Bradley with important input from

Ira Wyche, commander of the 79th Infantry Division, and General Eisenhower.

The 8th Infantry Division on the move near Folligny. NATIONAL ARCHIVES

Lightning Joe Collins—envisioned a massive effort on a narrow front of just four miles. Carpet bombing of German positions would precede a multi-division, multi-phase offensive commanded by Collins and intended to punch a hole in the enemy line while many German units were held in place at Caen by the just-concluded Operation Goodwood. By this time, American engineers and armored soldiers had devised a "solution" to the hedgerows: the Culin hedgerow cutter, or "Rhino," a set of steel teeth attached to the fronts of tanks that could plough through the hedges. Its debut would take place during

Cobra. Many of the tanks in the vanguard would be fitted with Rhinos, most of which, ironically, had been built from steel salvaged from German obstacles on the beaches.

After a false start on July 24, when Allied aircraft took off but were recalled because of bad weather (not before dropping bombs that killed several dozen Americans), Cobra began on July 25 with an aerial bombardment of epic proportions. That morning, 600 fighter-bombers attacked first, followed by more than 1,500 bombers, dropping 3,300 tons of bombs on a 3.5-by-1.25-mile rectangle west of St. Lô. (Misdrops

U.S. First Army (Bradley)
  VII Corps (Collins)
    1st Infantry Division
    2nd Armored Division
    3rd Armored Division
    4th Infantry Division
    9th Infantry Division
    30th Infantry Division
  VIII Corps (Middleton)
    4th Armored Division
    6th Armored Division
    8th Infantry Division
    79th Infantry Division
    83rd Infantry Division
    90th Infantry Division
  XIX Corps (Corlett)
    28th Infantry Division
    29th Infantry Division
    35th Infantry Division

killed more than 100 and wounded nearly 500 Americans. Among the dead was Gen. Lesley McNair, until recently the head of U.S. Army Ground Forces, the organization responsible for the raising and training of American combat divisions, and at his death commander of the fictional First U.S. Army Group. McNair was the highest-ranking American soldier to be killed in Europe.) The effects of the bombing were pulverizing, though not entirely paralyzing. For instance, the always-dangerous Panzer Lehr Division had been shaken but remained a cohesive fighting force, and enough pockets of German resistance remained to give American commanders pause. Notwithstanding the mixed results of the first day in the ground units, General Collins decided to go forward as planned with an attack the next day, spearheaded by the 2nd Armored Division and the 1st Infantry Division.

It was the right call. German defenses crumbled and then cracked wide open under the weight of

American armor and infantry, at last free to maneuver as they were trained to do. By July 28, the 4th Armored Division under "Tiger Jack" Wood took Coutances, fifteen miles away. Two days later, Wood's 4th, joined by the 6th Armored, captured Avranches, twenty-five miles south of Coutances.

The stalemate was over. It was time for a war of movement.

Enter Patton

June 1944 passed agonizingly slowly for Gen. George S. Patton. Before and after D-Day, he continued to perform vital service in the deception plan that placed him at the head of the phantom First U.S. Army Group (FUSAG) and aimed to confuse the Germans about the location of the main invasion. At the same time, he was preparing his Third Army, which he had officially commanded since January, and delivering various versions of the motivational speech made famous in the George C. Scott film. But Patton was champing at the bit to get into action and worried that the war would end before he could leave England and fulfill what he believed to be his destiny. He passed the time by studying the Normandy and Brittany campaigns of William the Conqueror.

You and I are the only people around here who seem to be enjoying this goddamned war."
➤ *George Patton to J. Lawton Collins*

Finally, on July 6, Patton arrived in France to begin readying the Third Army for future breakout operations. In command arrangements that would take effect on August 1, Patton would serve under Bradley, his former subordinate in North Africa and Sicily, who would command the new U.S. 12th Army Group. (Bradley's army group was numbered twelve to preserve the ruse of FUSAG.) American Courtney Hodges, a decorated World War I veteran and previously Bradley's deputy, would take over the First Army from Bradley. For now, until the preponderance of American forces in Europe made the arrangement no longer tenable, Montgomery would remain overall ground commander as well as commander of the British-Canadian 21st Army Group.

On August 1, a week after Cobra broke through the German front, Patton's Third Army began streaming through the Avranches gateway—some 100,000 men in a few days, quite a feat even if Cobra had paved the way. Part of the army turned to the west into Brittany (the

Soldiers of the 1st
Infantry Division
enjoy a lighter moment
near Caumont.
NATIONAL ARCHIVES

The 79th Infantry Division
recreates combat action
for the camera.
NATIONAL ARCHIVES

Artillery at work:
reloading a
105-millimeter gun.
NATIONAL ARCHIVES

Vital work: bombing rail lines. NATIONAL ARCHIVES

so-called "right turn"), targeting the ports of St. Malo, Brest, Lorient, and St. Nazaire. The Overlord plan stipulated their capture, and Bradley, mindful of supply concerns, was unwilling to deviate from that plan even though Cherbourg had not worked out as planned. St. Malo fell to the Americans on August 17, Brest only on September 19 (after the Germans had wrecked the port); Lorient and St. Nazaire held out until war's end. Historians continue to debate the wisdom of the Brittany operation.

Meanwhile, the rest of the Third Army turned east and southeast into the Germans' rear: one corps toward Le Mans, which was reached on August 8, and another toward the Loire River, which was reached on August 11.

We are advancing constantly, and we're not interested in holding on to anything."

> *George Patton*

Patton's Third Army had an impressive debut, from Avranches to Brittany to the Loire. At least one historian has called its actions *Blitzkrieg*. An officer in the Third Army compared the operation to a bomb exploding in the heart of France. With some soon-to-come and unintended assistance from the Germans, the Third Army's drive beyond Avranches was about to help create for the Allies, as General Bradley put it, "an opportunity that comes to a commander not more than once in a century … to destroy an entire hostile army."

George S. Patton Career Highlights

1885	Born in California
1903–4	Attends Virginia Military Institute
1909	Graduates from West Point (46 of 103)
1912	Olympic Games (modern pentathlon)
1913	U.S. Army's "Master of the Sword"
1915–17	Mexican border, including Pancho Villa Expedition
1917–18	World War I:
	Aide to General Pershing in Europe
	Establishes Light Tank School
	Commands 304th Tank Brigade
	Battle of St. Mihiel
	Wounded in Meuse-Argonne Offensive
1925–27	Personnel/intelligence/operations officer, Hawaiian Division
1927–31	Office of the Chief of Cavalry
1931–32	Army War College
1932	Leads 3rd Cavalry in "Bonus Army" action in Washington, DC
1934–37	Intelligence officer, Hawaiian Division
1938	Commander, 5th Cavalry
1938–39	Commander, 3rd Cavalry
1940	Promoted to brigadier general
1941	Commander, 2nd Armored Division
1942	Commander, I Armored Corps
	Establishes Desert Training Center
	Commands Western Task Force, Operation Torch
1943	Commands II Corps, Tunisian Campaign
	Commands Seventh Army, Sicilian Campaign
	Slaps two soldiers on Sicily
1944	"Commander," fictional First U.S. Army Group
1944–45	Commander, Third Army: Normandy breakout, Lorraine, the Bulge, Germany
1945	Military governor of Bavaria
	Commander, Fifteenth U.S. Army
	Dies two weeks after car crash in Germany

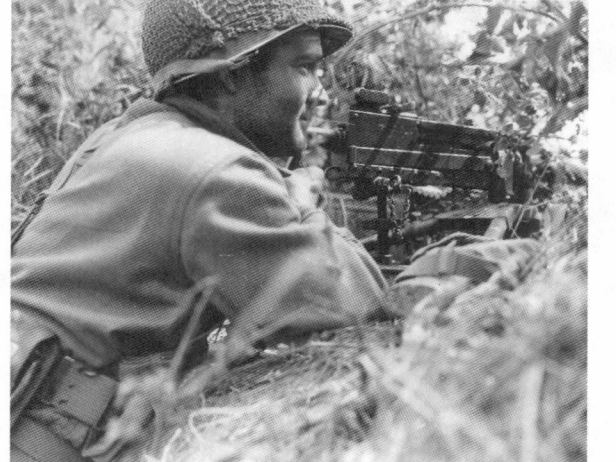

A soldier mans an M1919 Browning machine gun. NATIONAL ARCHIVES

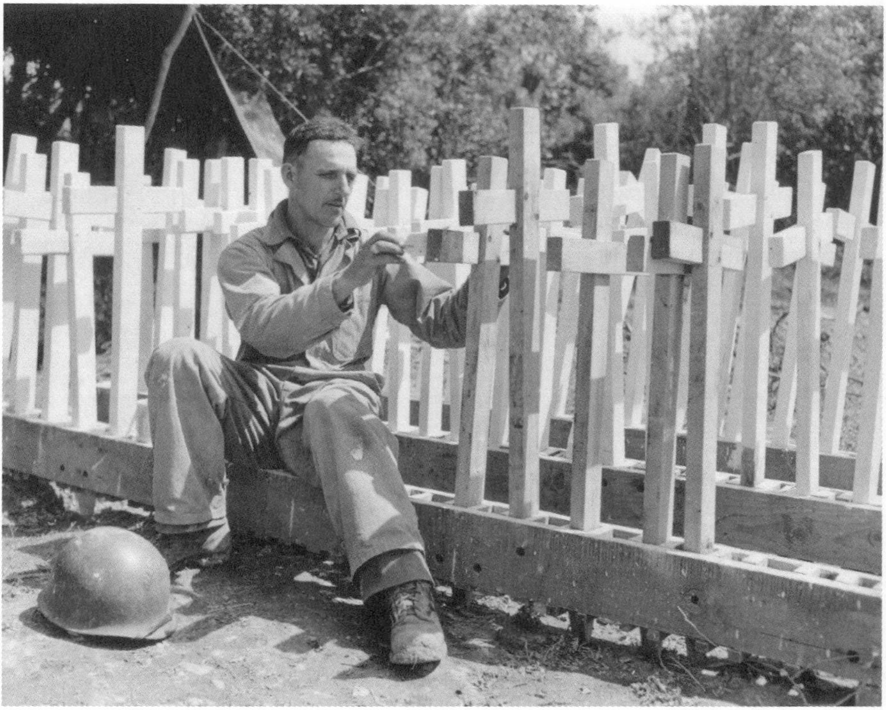

A graves registration soldier prepares crosses for the cemetery behind Omaha Beach. NATIONAL ARCHIVES

The Germans Strike Back

July was a dark month for Nazi Germany. On June 22, the third anniversary of Operation Barbarossa, the Soviets launched Operation Bagration, the major offensive Stalin had promised Roosevelt and Churchill at Tehran. The Red Army committed approximately two million men and literally wiped German armies off the map. By August 19, the Soviets had inflicted 400,000 casualties and were at the doorstep of Warsaw.

In Normandy, the Allies had a beachhead from which they almost surely could not be dislodged; Cherbourg, which Hitler had wanted held at all costs, had surrendered; and by the start of July's third week, with the fall of Caen and St. Lô, the Allies were beginning to break the stalemate. The German commanders in Normandy, Rundstedt and Rommel, sought permission to order local withdrawals, which Hitler denied—and soon thereafter replaced Rundstedt with Günther von Kluge as Commander-in-Chief West. A Prussian aristocrat like Rundstedt, Kluge had commanded an army in the invasions of Poland, France, and the Soviet Union, where he went on to lead an army group and also accepted a 250,000 Reichsmark reward—really a bribe for his loyalty—from Hitler. Injured in a car accident in October 1943, Kluge returned to duty to replace Rundstedt. Two weeks later, on July 17, a Spitfire fighter strafed Rommel's car, causing a crash that fractured the field marshal's skull. Kluge would also head Rommel's army group.

For years, a tiny element within the German Army had been conspiring against Hitler and awaiting the right moment to take action. That moment seemed to have come during the summer of 1944, as the Third Reich's military fortunes waned. On July 20, at a meeting at Hitler's Wolf's Lair headquarters, Col. Claus von Stauffenberg placed a briefcase bomb under the table and excused himself. Minutes later, an explosion blasted the room, killing four. Protected by a table leg that blocked part of the blast, Hitler survived—and launched a ruthless investigation to eliminate the conspirators. Under suspicion were Rommel, still in the hospital with serious injuries, and Kluge.

On August 2, with part of the German front collapsing and Patton's Third Army racing through Avranches, Hitler ordered Kluge to mount an armored counter-offensive—"like lightning"—from Mortain west through Avranches to the sea, hitting the southward-attacking Americans in their flank and cutting off the Third Army. Kluge recognized that the German situation was increasingly untenable—indeed, he advocated a withdrawal to the Seine—and knew Hitler's plan was folly: rather than endangering Patton's army, the counteroffensive was more likely to thrust German forces out in front of their main line and risk their being trapped by a north–south Allied pincer, with the Third Army representing the southern "jaw." But Kluge, suspected in the July 20 plot, was in no position to disobey.

I f, as I foresee, this plan does not succeed, catastrophe is inevitable."

➤ *Günther von Kluge on Lüttich*

Operation Lüttich—also known as the Mortain counterattack—stepped off on the night of August 6 without a preceding artillery bombardment to maintain surprise that had already been lost: thanks to Ultra, the Allies had been decrypting German communications for many months, and they knew the Germans were preparing to attack. By the morning of the seventh, some panzer units had pushed up to seven miles west of Mortain, but they were halted by Allied armor and punishing air attacks.

Two infantrymen take a break to eat and sleep. NATIONAL ARCHIVES

Above: Soldiers of the
2nd Armored Division
with German prisoners.
NATIONAL ARCHIVES

Right: A tankman of the
2nd Armored Division
pauses for a meal.
NATIONAL ARCHIVES

Falaise–Argentan

Now the Allies had a chance to bag a significant portion of the German army. On August 7–8, the Canadians mounted a previously planned offensive south of Caen (Operation Totalize), aiming for Falaise, and on the eighth, forces of Patton's Third Army reached Le Mans. If the Canadians could take Falaise and if Patton advanced north from Le Mans to Alençon, the Allies would be a town away—Argentan—from pinching off a pocket containing some 100,000 Germans engaged around Mortain. Allied plans had called for a wide envelopment, swinging down along the Loire River and hooking northeast toward Orleans and Paris. But Eisenhower, Montgomery, and Bradley agreed that the battlefield situation now called for a shorter envelopment focusing on Falaise, Argentan, and Alençon.

L et's talk big turkey. I'm ready to eat meat all the way."
> *Omar Bradley on Falaise–Argentan*

The Canadians fought with a vengeance in Operation Totalize, the inaugural operation of the First Canadian Army, which included not only a Canadian but also a Polish armored division. The 12th SS Panzer Division "Hitler Youth" had massacred Canadian soldiers at Ardenne Abbey, and the exiled Poles knew how the Germans had ravaged their country and its people —and were ravaging it still, now in the Warsaw Uprising. Neither the Canadians nor the Poles were inclined to tread lightly. Even so, the going was tough for the First

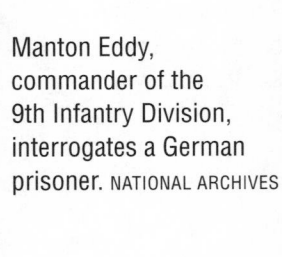

Manton Eddy, commander of the 9th Infantry Division, interrogates a German prisoner. NATIONAL ARCHIVES

On the lookout near Chambois. NATIONAL ARCHIVES

Canadian Army, which, despite high fighting spirit, showed signs of inexperience in the two armored divisions. By August 10, the Canadians were still eight miles short of Falaise. (As small consolation, the operation yielded a notable kill: tank ace Michael Wittmann, German hero of Villers-Bocage, whose Tiger was ambushed and destroyed by a host of Shermans.)

To the south, the Third Army drove north from Le Mans, passed through Alençon, and by August 12 threatened Argentan. Here Patton's vanguard ran against the boundary between the American and British-Canadian sectors. Bradley was unwilling to seek the movement of that boundary, fearing that the Americans coming from the south could collide with the Canadians coming from the north, and, more significantly, that a push to Falaise would dangerously overstretch Patton's line and invite disaster if the Germans attempted to fight their way out of the pocket as the Mortain counteroffensive crumbled. Said Bradley: "I much preferred a solid shoulder at Argentan to the possibility of a broken neck at Falaise." He ordered a halt, one of the campaign's most controversial decisions. The gap remained open.

We now have elements in Argentan. Shall we continue and drive the British into the sea for another Dunkirk?"

> *George Patton*

Armored scout car at the Arc de Triomphe. NATIONAL ARCHIVES

On August 14, while the Canadians renewed their offensive to take Falaise (Operation Tractable), Bradley turned Patton loose in a drive for the Seine River that was closer in design to the wider envelopment of the Allies' original plans. Patton's army raced east from Argentan and

     THE NORMANDY CAMPAIGN

Kluge's Last Letter

Günther von Kluge wrote Hitler a final letter before taking his life:

When you receive these lines, I shall be no more. I cannot bear that criticism that I have sealed the fate of the west through faulty strategy; and I have no means of defending myself. I have drawn my conclusions from that and am sending myself where thousands of my comrades already lie. I have never feared death. Life has no more meaning for me. . . .

Mein Führer, I think I can say that I did everything I could to keep on top of the situation. Rommel, myself, and probably all the commanders in the west, who know what it is to fight the Anglo-Americans with their overwhelming material superiority, foresaw current developments. No one listened to us. Our appreciations were not dictated by pessimism, rather from a sober assessment of the situation. I do not know whether Field Marshal Model will be able to master the situation. In my heart, I hope he will. But if he cannot . . . then make up your mind to end the war. The German people have borne untold suffering, it is time to put an end to this misery. ■

Le Mans and was more than half-way to the river within two or three days, having reached Dreux, Chartres, and Orleans. On August 15, in Operation Dragoon, the Allies began landing forces in southern France for an offensive north from Marseille to Lyon and Dijon. On August 16, Canadian forces entered Falaise. The noose was tightening around the Germans.

The German counteroffensive at Mortain had petered out in the Allies' jaws, and despite the untenable situation, Hitler, who kept a tight rein on operations from his headquarters in Germany, insisted

on continuing the attack, which at this point was not folly but fantasy. Kluge understood the direness but, given his connection to the July 20 attempted coup, had no strength with which to oppose Hitler—and might even save himself by carrying out the Fürher's absurd orders. When Hitler recalled him to Germany on August 15, Kluge knew the game was up. He swallowed cyanide en route. (Rommel did the same two months later.)

To replace Kluge, Hitler selected Walter Model. Wounded in the First World War, Model distinguished himself during the 1940 Battle of

France and fought on the Eastern Front from 1941. There he earned a reputation as a tenacious commander, especially skilled in the defensive warfare the Germans had to conduct more and more from 1942. So talented was he that he became Hitler's "fireman," tasked with breaking out of encirclements and mounting counteroffensives. Most recently he had scored modest success against the Soviets' Operation Bagration. Hitler hoped Model could work his magic in Normandy.

But the German front was deteriorating too rapidly for Model to be able to do much, although he did succeed where Kluge had failed in convincing Hitler to allow a withdrawal out of the Falaise pocket and retreat to the Seine—which saved many thousands of German soldiers before the gap was finally sealed shut on August 21, trapping as many as 50,000 Germans in an area littered with corpses, dead animals, burnt-out vehicles, and discarded equipment. The Falaise pocket had become a burning, stinking, horrifying hell.

> **S**cenes that could be described only by Dante. It was literally possible to walk for hundreds of yards at a time, stepping on nothing but dead and decaying flesh."
>
> ➤ *Dwight Eisenhower on the Falaise pocket*

The End of the Normandy Campaign

While the Falaise pocket was being closed, elements of Patton's Third Army reached the Seine northwest and southeast of Paris, crossing at Mantes. Over the next week, more Americans and other Allied forces crossed the river but were unable to cut off the retreating Germans, who fell back beyond the Seine to ports on the English Channel and to a series of river lines starting with the Somme and Marne and moving eastward toward Luxembourg, Belgium, and Germany. Some 250,000 troops had made it out of Normandy, leaving behind most of their precious tanks, and Model was reconstituting them into a cohesive army, supplemented by any reinforcements that could be scraped together. In what history has termed the "Miracle in the West," the Germans survived to fight another day—many more days, in fact.

Charles de Gaulle Addresses Liberated Paris, August 25, 1944

Paris! Paris outraged! Paris broken! Paris martyred! But Paris liberated! Liberated by itself, liberated by its people with the help of the French armies, with the support and the help of all France—of the France that fights, of the only France, of the real France, of the eternal France!

Well! Since the enemy which held Paris has capitulated into our hands, France returns to Paris, to her home. She returns bloody but resolute. She returns enlightened by this immense lesson, but more certain than ever of her duties and her rights. . . .

The enemy is staggering, but he is not beaten yet. He remains on our soil. It will not be enough that we have, with the help of our dear and admirable allies, chased him from our country. . . . We want to enter his country as is fitting—as victors.

This is why the French vanguard has entered Paris with guns blazing. This is why the great French army from Italy has landed in the south and is advancing rapidly up the Rhône valley. This is why our brave and dear Forces of the Interior will arm themselves with modern weapons. It is for this revenge, this vengeance and justice, that we will keep fighting until the final day, until the day of total and complete victory. . . .

Vive la France! ∎

Today I spat in the Seine."

> ➤ *George Patton to Dwight Eisenhower*

Allied planners had envisioned liberating Paris later. Capturing it presented a range of problems, from the military difficulty of taking an urban garrison to concerns about wrecking the city and supplying the civilian population after liberation. Once the Germans were in retreat, however, the people of Paris rose up, first with strikes and then with attacks on the occupiers: snipers, mines, barricades, bombs. Hitler called for the city's destruction: "Is Paris burning?" he asked his commander in Paris. The Allies could hold off no longer. Eisenhower released the French 2nd Armored Division, which entered Paris on August 24. Surrender came the following day.

The Axis in Retreat: Other Events during the Normandy Campaign

June 15–July 9	Battle of Saipan
June 22	Operation Bagration launched by Red Army
	Battle of Kohima ends
July 3	Battle of Imphal ends
July 20	Attempted assassination of Adolf Hitler
July 21–Aug 10	Battle of Guam
July 24	Red Army liberates Majdanek concentration camp
July 24–Aug 1	Battle of Tinian
Aug 1–Oct 2	Warsaw Uprising
Aug 3	Allies take Myitkyina in Burma, open Ledo Road
Aug 15	Operation Dragoon begins in southern France
Aug 23	Romania surrenders to Soviet Union
Aug 25	Allies launch offensive against Gothic Line in Italy

Two and a half months of bitter fighting, culminating for the Germans in a blood-bath big enough even for their extravagant tastes, have brought the end of the war in Europe within sight."

> ➤ *SHAEF report, August 26*

From D-Day to the closing of the Falaise gap, more than two million Allied soldiers landed in France. Of them, more than 200,000 became casualties. Allied air forces flew nearly half a million sorties. The Germans committed more than 600,000 men to the campaign and lost over half that number killed, wounded, and captured.

The Allies had liberated a vast portion of France and secured a lodgment from which the invasion of Germany could be launched. By the middle of September, Allied troops were approaching the German frontier five months ahead of schedule. Roosevelt and Churchill met once again in Quebec, where they agreed to shift some resources to the Pacific and made plans for postwar Germany. Euphoria swept Allied armies, from foot soldiers to high command. The end of the war seemed in sight—weeks, some said, or at least by Christmas.

Four days after the liberation of Paris, the U.S. 28th Infantry Division marched in a parade at the Arc de Triomphe in Paris. Veterans of the Normandy campaign, the men of the Keystone Division did not know that defeating Nazi Germany would take another eight months of grueling, grinding, slogging combat. More men—men not even in Europe yet—would die in more battles: the Siegfried Line, the Hürtgen Forest, the Battle of the Bulge, the Rhine. For the 28th, as for many other divisions, its most difficult battles lay ahead.

Normandy was but the beginning.

Heading home. A paratrooper of the 82nd Airborne prepares to leave Normandy. NATIONAL ARCHIVES

The 28th Infantry Division parades in Paris, August 29, 1944. NATIONAL ARCHIVES

THE NORMANDY CAMPAIGN

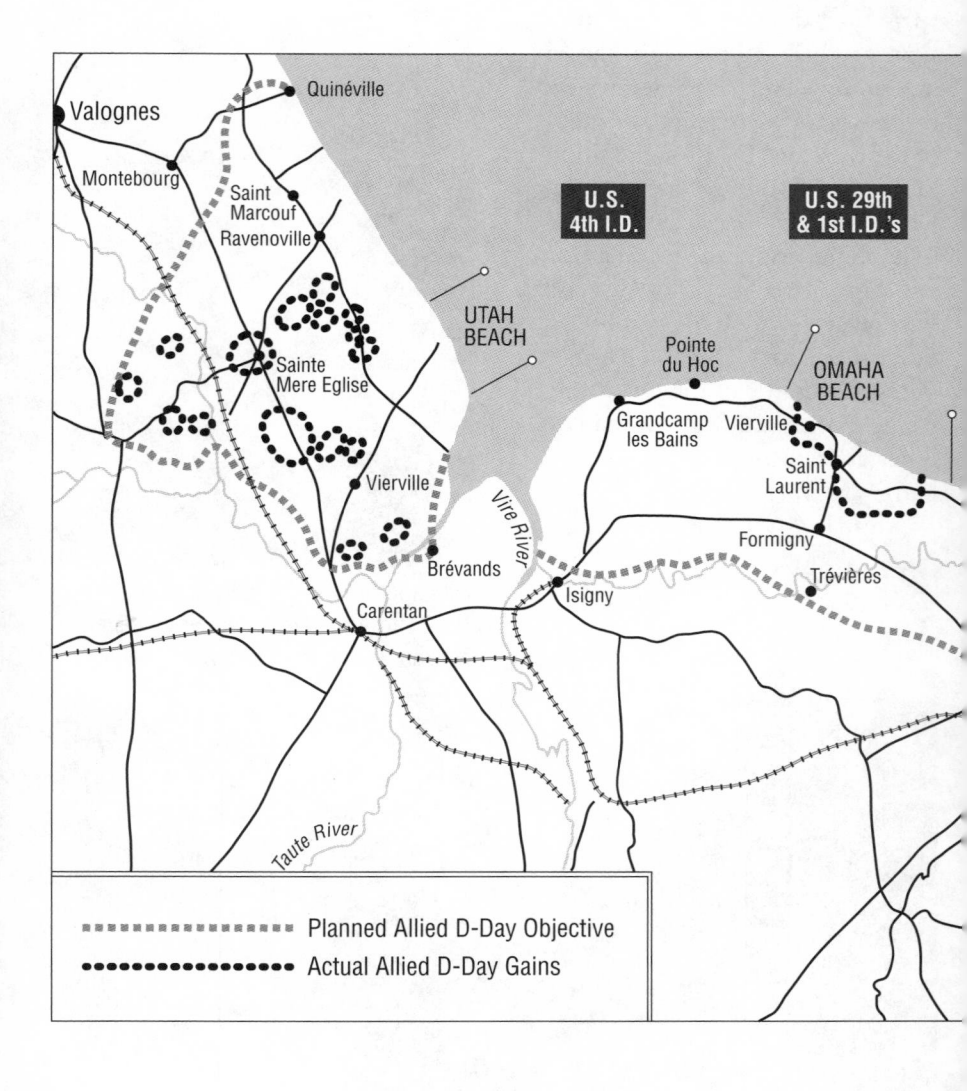

Valognes

Quinéville

Montebourg

Saint
Marcouf
Ravenoville

Sainte
Mere Eglise

Vierville

U.S.
4th I.D.

UTAH
BEACH

Pointe
du Hoc

Grandcamp
les Bains

Vierville

U.S. 29th
& 1st I.D.'s

OMAHA
BEACH

Saint
Laurent

Brévands

Vire River

Formigny

Trévières

Carentan

Isigny

Taute River

Planned Allied D-Day Objective

Actual Allied D-Day Gains

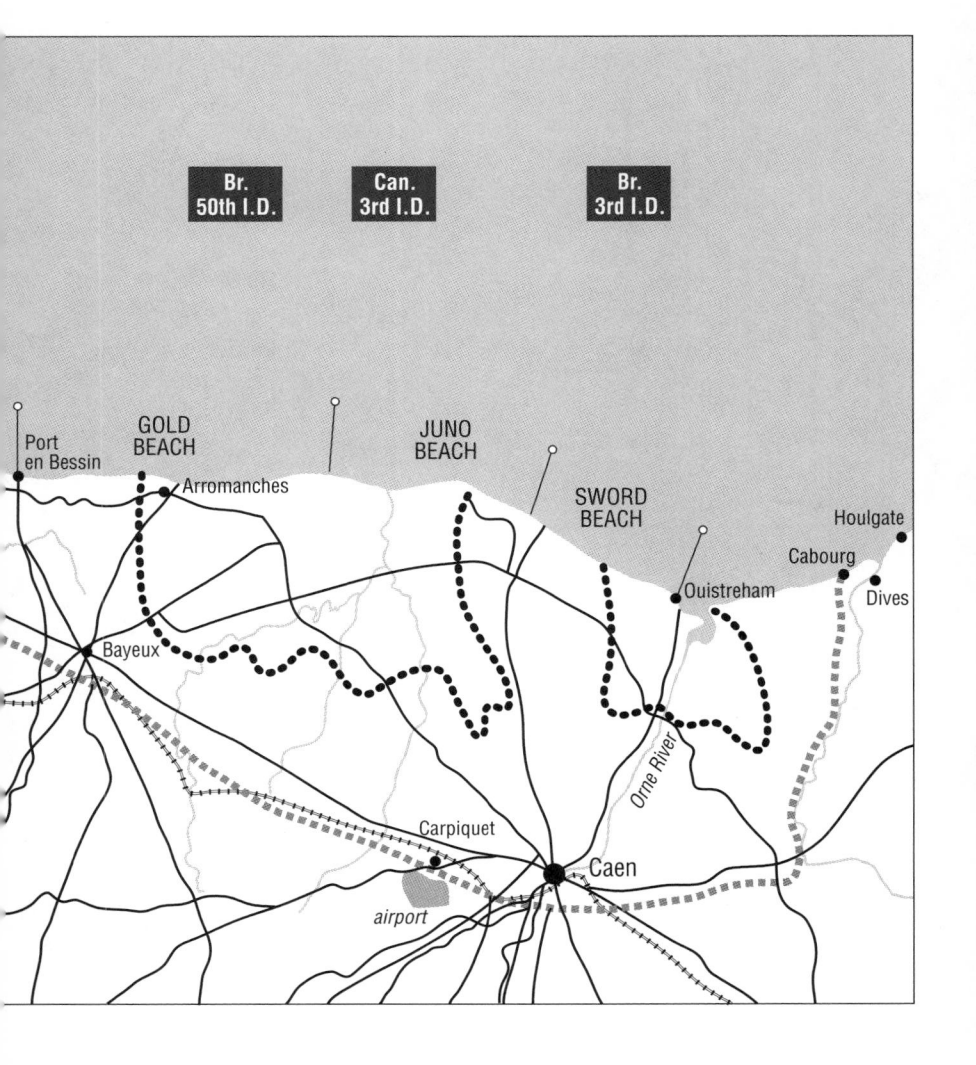

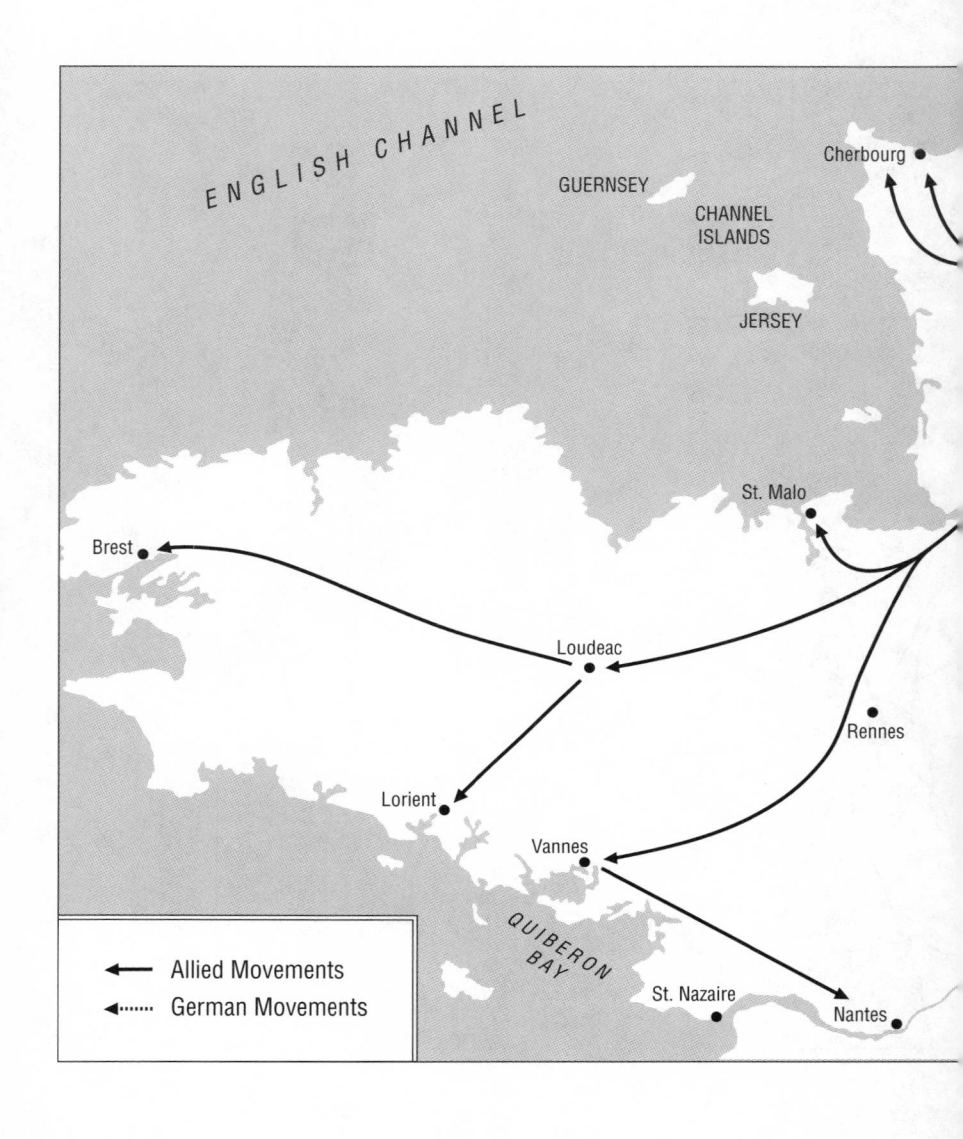

ENGLISH CHANNEL

GUERNSEY

CHANNEL
ISLANDS

Cherbourg

JERSEY

St. Malo

Brest

Loudeac

Rennes

Lorient

Vannes

QUIBERON
BAY

St. Nazaire

Nantes

→ Allied Movements
◄······ German Movements

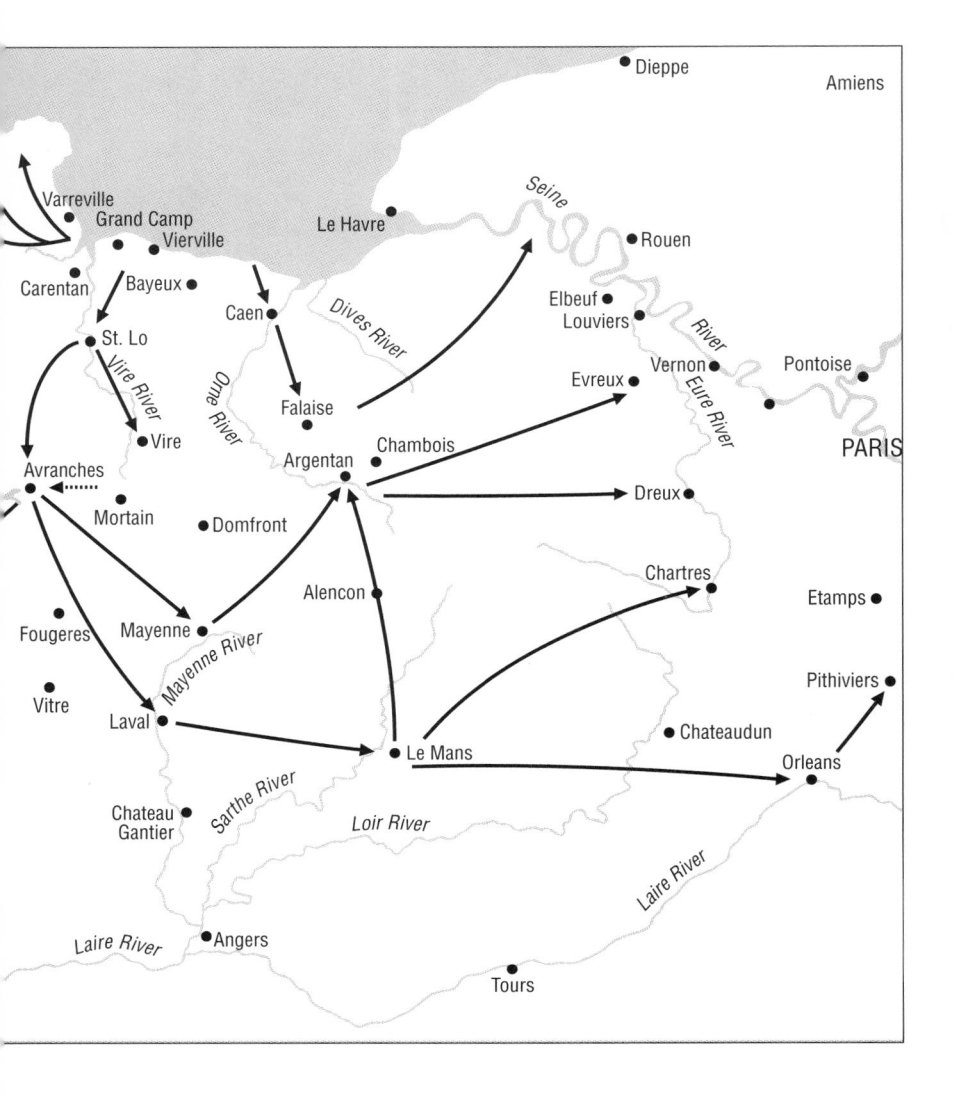

Dieppe

Amiens

Varreville
Grand Camp
Vierville
Le Havre

Seine

Rouen

Carentan
Bayeux

Caen

Dives River

Elbeuf
Louviers

River

St. Lo

Vire River

Vire

Ornes River

Falaise

Avranches

Mortain

Domfront

Argentan

Chambois

Vernon

Pontoise

PARIS

Evreux

Eure River

Dreux

Fougeres

Mayenne

Alencon

Chartres

Etamps

Vitre

Mayenne River

Laval

Le Mans

Pithiviers

Chateau
Gantier

Sarthe River

Chateaudun

Orleans

Loir River

Laire River

Laire River

Angers

Tours

An Army at Dawn, The Day of Battle, and *The Guns at Last Light* by Rick Atkinson. The Liberation Trilogy does for World War II what Bruce Catton did for the Civil War.

Beyond the Beachhead by Joseph Balkoski. The classic account of an American division in Normandy: its landing on Omaha Beach, hedgerow fighting, and the battle for St. Lô.

Churchill, Roosevelt & Company by Lewis E. Lehrman. Carefully researched analysis of the men, from diplomats to generals, who made the alliance work (and sometimes not).

Closing with the Enemy by Michael Doubler. Thoughtful examination of how the U.S. fighting man mastered the tactical challenges of the war (including the *bocage*) and became a formidable fighting force.

The Devil's Garden by Steven Zaloga. How the Germans defended Normandy, with special emphasis on how those defenses made the Allied advance difficult at Omaha Beach.

Eisenhower by Carlo D'Este. Essential military biography of the essential commander.

Eisenhower's Lieutenants by Russell F. Weigley. Masterful history of the U.S. Army's war in Europe, from D-Day through VE-Day.

The Longest Day by Cornelius Ryan. Painstaking recreation of D-Day, based on a massive assembly of interviews; one of the first and still one of the best.

Omaha Beach and *Utah Beach* by Joseph Balkoski. Taken together, these books present as complete a picture of the Americans on D-Day as we are likely to get.

Overlord by Max Hastings. Vivid, compact narrative covering all sides from D-Day to Falaise, with evocative firsthand descriptions throughout.

Six Armies in Normandy by John Keegan. The campaign from the perspective of the Americans, British, Canadians, French, Poles, and Germans.

A World at Arms by Gerhard Weinberg. The gold standard in one-volume histories of the war, combining diplomatic, military, political, and economic perspectives.